## ALSO BY
## ANGELICA EBERLE

Are You

Are You Ready for a Miracle?
with Chiropractic

Are You Ready For a Miracle?
with Herbs And Vitamins

Are You Ready For a Miracle?
for Addiction

Are You Ready For A Miracle?
for Children Of All Ages

Are You Ready For A Miracle?
for The Entrepreneur

Are You Ready for a Miracle?
for Lovers

Shameless Self Promotion—
The American Way

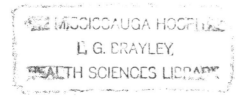
Gift of Random House

# Secrets of Success

Excellence :
The Chosen Path

# By Angelica Eberle Wagner

Dreamakers International Inc.

# Secrets of Success

Excellence :
The Chosen Path

# By Angelica Eberle Wagner

Dreamakers International Inc.

Canadian Cataloguing in Publication Data

Wagner, Angelica, 1952-
    Secrets of success

ISBN 1-896375-01-4

1. Success in business.      I. Title

HFS386.W33   1997          650.1          C97-931126-8


First Printing May 1997

Cover and interior book design/art prodcution:
Karen Petherick, Petherick & Associates, Markham, Ontario,
Division of BIA Communications Limited

Printed and bound in Canada by:
Webcom Limited

*To my father:*
Alexander Zeeb,
maverick, revolutionary, entrepreneur,
who taught me the basics of business when I could read.

*To my mentors:*
Who lifted me on their shoulders so I could see further:
Suzanne Banfield Lount
Greg Gilmour
Glenn Ponomarenko
Brian Tracey
Leland Val Van de Wall

*To my wonderful children*:
who taught me humor,
when dreams took time to be realities:
Jennifer, Andrea, Jake and Lauren

# GRATEFUL ACKNOWLEDGEMENTS

I am deeply grateful to my team whose energy, enthusiasm, and inspiration transformed the vision of this book into reality.

Your commitment to purpose made the difference.

To Marilyn G. Richardson: Thank you for your endless support and tireless encouragement through times of victory and times we could not see progress.

To Karen Petherick: For you interior design, cover brilliance and knowing innately how to project the message with style. Your amazing efforts at "miracle making" kept us on time.

To Bill Belfontaine: For your belief in my work in publishing and book management. Thank you.

To my mentors: Leland Val Van de Wall, Brian Tracey, Suzanne Banfield Lount, Glenn Ponomarenko, and Greg Gilmour; your input and direction led my footsteps in the paths of excellence.

To my colleagues and friends at Re/Max Realty Specialists Inc. for whom this book was written to thank you for your encouragement and support in all my endeavours.

To Mark Victor Hansen, Thomas T. Tierney, Dave Liniger, my corporate friends at Reimer Express, General Motors, C.P.Rail, C.N. Rail, Nabisco, Dupont, Bodywise Int. Inc., AMJ Campbell and the many corporations I have served over the years.

# Table of Contents

# Secrets

# Table of Contents

# Table of Contents

*Chapter One*

# EXCELLENCE
## *The Chosen Path*

ONEY IS NOT ENOUGH REASON TO DO ANYTHING. In the final analysis, it is the least acceptable reason for existence, because life will pay you whatever amount you demand of it, if you demand enough of yourself to give the very best. It is in the heart energy of our very fiber as humans the real wealth lies—there in your interpretation of the universe and your attitude of gratitude are the events that will shape your own destiny. Society may predict, but only you can determine your ultimate destiny.

Does it begin with wealth, a good family, emotional support, caring co-workers? Those are wonderful ingredients if you can begin with them, the truth being the most spectacular success stories began with lives that were tattered, imperfect, dysfunctional relationships, and co-workers never looked back to see who they stepped on in their climb to the top of the ladder.

George Bernard Shaw wrote: "The reasonable man adapts himself to the world, the unreasonable one persists in trying to adapt the world to himself. Therefore, all progress depends on the unreasonable man." This book is a small guide to being unreasonable in a reasonable world, to implementing strategies that work, are time specific, and create change in your business world and hopefully, the quality of your life. It is in the way that we interpret the world that our future is found. The decision to make change is your own. The decision to implement involves being unreasonable in your expectations of yourself.

This is not a cultural neurosis of this time. The soul that is shattered in pain is not suffering from neurosis. It is suffering from the pain of reality. Whether this is the individual soul or the collective soul of a corporation, the pain is real. Yet, the hungry state of passionate expectation of greatness and the internal certainty of success are the key ingredients that lead our lives to greatness and ultimately shape our destiny. Only you are responsible for the quality of your own life.

Being outstanding is not a skill–it is only heart. There the true energy is found. In the willingness to contribute, to make a difference to society, to commit to excellence, there lies the magical path to success. It is found in each without compromise of integrity or standards of performance. If anything; heart takes us to places of performance that could never be found through intellect or reason alone. It takes us out of and beyond ourselves into the never-never land of return—that of making a contribution to society.

Excellence the chosen path, the stepping stones to greatness are found in every day tasks. In the book *In Search of Excellence*, Waterman and Peters have given us something to believe in, something to commit to, and something that gives us meaning for existence in our own realities. The word "excellence" transforms us, not just because it bridges the gap between what is done and what must be done, but also sets compelling values. Meaningful work raises the standard from what we currently expect to what is unexpected—a standard of superior performance. Contributing to excellence every day transforms all interaction and captures the magic of our existence.

Studies done in both Canada and the United States on the best run companies have found that the winners had long standing records of successful innovation in responding to the trends in the market place. Corporate surveys show that the following techniques have been mastered whether they are Canadian or American companies.

1.  Supporting risk through action and interpretation.
2.  Full partnership and interaction with the client or customer.
3.  Stimulating individual innovation and entrepreneurship within the ranks.
4.  Motivating people to choose productivity for their own benefit.
5.  Hands-on management to shape value systems.
6.  Letting management manage due to simplification of structures and lean support staff.
7.  Releasing latent potential in staff by providing the parameters for control in the values that are set.

These dynamic companies also provided:

1.  Leadership with compelling, mobilizing vision.
2.  Liberating talent while supporting the value systems and controls.
3.  Leadership with extensive experience and knowledge of industry operations.

These fundamentals of business were found in the underlying need for each person to find meaning in the corporate existence. Excellence was found in people with ordinary human needs—the need to want to make a difference. These bodies in the whole corporate body contributed exceptional energies, displayed unexpected wisdom and talent when given a reason to have something worthwhile in which to belong. It became, in essence, a chance to shape their own destiny.

These are the stepping stones to greatness.

Excellence displayed in the corporate body became the work of the human soul. The corporate body showed the same opportunities for progress and growth as the physical body—enhanced throughout the collective collaboration of many minds.

### Characteristics of excellent companies

* Leadership with a clear compelling vision
* Balancing the liberation of talent with support from within the ranks
* Industry leadership – experience created through the good and the bad.

Commitment to these basic fundamentals of business were found in the underlying need for each person within the corporation to find meaning. Excellence was found in very ordinary people because of their human needs. These people contributed exceptional energies and displayed unexpected wisdom and incredible talent when belonging to something worthwhile, and being given the chance to shape their destiny in the context of their field of endeavor.

Excellence clearly displayed by you is the art of the human soul embodied in the character of work.

## *Leadership*

1. Having a clear, compelling vision of their work.
2. Having both plans and systems and sticking to them no matter what.
3. Hunger to be number 1 in the industry.
4. Delivered superior value to customers/clients from the first interaction.
5. Key to successful business was not only in the numbers, but in how you treated people . . . it was that simple.
6. Reason for being went beyond the financial into providing value not just for the customer, but also for the community.
7. Focusing on the business they knew best.
8. Being the industry leader was the only way the business operated.

Without clear vision and reason for being within your corporation or even your mini-corporation (yourself), you may as well fold your tent and leave town. It is the clear uncompromising vision of the future that will predetermine the results of your efforts.

- What is your vision?
- What is your dream?
- What is your purpose?

### *Balancing Liberation of Talent with Support*

1. Successful people are not necessarily more talented, they are more committed.
2. Take a basic set of values and get on with the business of growing upward in your corporation.
3. Managers need the freedom to make a few wrong decisions and recognize them as learning tools.

4. Keep people involved and motivated.
5. Recognition and awards to the staff are the keys to superior growth in any company.
6. Commitment to hard, tough, budgeting—everything is based on profit-centered thinking .
7. Energy is created and directed within the essentials of the business and the external environment of their community.

In understanding ourselves and our needs we can best direct our efforts into creating motivating behaviors. The psychologist, Ernest Beeker said, "Man is driven by being a member of a winning team as well as being a star in his own right."

I often wonder whether corporations encourage "stardom" or "boredom" in their talented people.

Liberation of talent is a key in any business. The mavericks that kick up dust always show more commitment to result than they do to process. When dealing with these people and their ideas, it is really best to have an open mind and a closed mouth. They will find ways to accomplish goals within companies in creative ways, not necessarily following the norm. These mavericks are driven by their own visionary energy. If you observe their methods, they will seem to unfold for you from the inside out and usually in a non-linear style—that is they will not proceed through point a to b to c to d to e. You will find they jump all over the globe in both thought and procedure more like a to k to v to s to o.

In the end, the results often are amazing. Allow the mavericks the space and room that they need to grow.

Mavericks need reward rather than punishment. Their style is unconventional, their results always superior.

Without the hurricane of this visionary energy and

reason for being, the energy of the company and its members will slowly evaporate like water on the road on a hot summer's day. Visionary, compelling energy forces growth, productivity, and life force throughout the body of a company.

## LEADERSHIP IN THE INDUSTRY

Leaders have the following characteristics:

- Many years of company and industry experience
- They feel the rhythm of the business; taking the good with the bad
- Top management has worked together for years and have established decision-making patterns
- Confidence allows companies to dialogue with both customers, competitors and employees; there is an equal exchange of information for the benefit of all.
- The prevailing mood is one of optimism and trust.

One of the key points to excellence has always been the cohesion of the team. This is not only found in the strength of management teams, but in the grass-roots belief in excellence on all levels; that the fiber of the company begins and ends in cohesive harmony based on trust. The questions to ask are:

- How strong is the management team in this organization?
- How unified is the management team in their decision making process?
- Is there enough room for varying opinions and the integration of these opinions into the final decision?

The employee, customer, or competitor who knows his concerns will be heard, understood, and fairly dealt with has a different type of dialogue than the one who has no trust. It takes more than a contract to keep employees today. It takes the belief and expressed concern that they matter.

Soul levels of integrity on all levels of responsibility are not a frivolous option. They are a requirement for the basis of opportunity.

### Balancing the process

Excellence, therefore, becomes an interactive flow of three variables:

1.  Pathfinding
2.  Decision Making
3.  Implementation

The interconnection of these core values and beliefs become harmony in planning and strategies. Excellent companies, excellent managers, excellent businesses all know how to live meaningful visions, to support risk in decision making, to encourage commitment in pulling together through the implementation process.

Why does excellence depend on meaning? The bottom line of the Kinsey report was that companies have to provide binding significance to their people. Creating visions of greatness, supported by entrepreneurial spirit, propels people to contribute their full talents and manage themselves for innovation, productivity, and quality.

The secret to success in the human experience is in the need to make a difference. Never underestimate how much this one point can matter.

At the most basic human level, making a difference in the community is important in the larger field of participation. In the examination of human needs and human existence, one addresses excellence within the organization according to the attributes of the living, breathing, human potential.

In learning to view the corporation in the context of the human organism, the depth, breadth and life of the company is reflected in the body, mind and spirit of an organism that requires energy and vitality.

The best ideas always come from the field. When you remove the interference in the nervous system of the human body, energy is created. When you remove the interference and resistance on the corporate level, you create Corporate Quantum Energy.

## *Excellent companies are what they talk about*

1. Encouraging the mavericks and the rebels to be their best.
2. Bootlegging; adapting or adopting ideas from each other and other companies. This is especially important when the industry is not in a growth stage.
3. Supporting and examining failed experiments, to see where more can be learned.
4. Honoring champions; those who keep getting up no matter how often life knocks them down.

Excellent companies need to be sailed not driven to superior performance. Achieving top performance depends on the talents of a disciplined crew and masterful adjustment of the sails to catch the most favourable winds of opportunity and the timing of the events. Honoring everyone's wisdom is at the soul of a growth oriented corporation.

Remembering that there is not just one wisdom but a unification of effort, function and production when everyone's effort and impact is requested and honored.

It supports the principles of the mastermind consequence, as well as showing the need to make a difference.

We are each inbred with the energy of our internal fires. The higher the output of energy, the greater the energy of the whole. This makes the corporation indivisible in unity and productivity. It is the unity of the top performers in any company that allows the corporation to sail through the troughs of depression and recession in any economy. If your company has been washed ashore with a broken rudder, look first at management:

- internal cohesion
- levels of integration
- levels of integrity of thought and production
- question personal vision in regard to purpose

When the organization is devoted to excellence, only then will commitment to the individual bloom and grow. The wisdom of the collective unity is the glue that firmly binds the result. Wasteland or oasis, the water is in your people.

*Chapter Two*

# EXCELLENCE
# IN YOUR PEOPLE
## *The Entrepreneur is You*

*E*xcellent companies, no matter what their size, always act like small companies. Not only do they look at internal cohesion of the teams:

- levels of integration of effort
- levels of integrity of thought
- personal vision as to purpose

they also understand that:

1. Self-initiated, self-directed experimentation is the key to success.
2. To create ownership, projects must be encouraged
3. The creative fanatic must not be tolerated, he must be encouraged
4. Creativity means dreaming up new things, innovation is doing old and new things better.
5. Power to implement these ideas is critical to entrepreneurism.

- No support systems for the people = no champions
- No champions = no change
- No innovation = no revolution

Inversion of the current paradigm is normal and expected for the entrepreneur. It all turns around for the rebel who wants to prove the idea will or will not work. Listening puts the rebel on a direct course for change and your company on a direct course for innovation and breaking through the financial barriers. **First, some decisions about values that are important.**

### *Factors that determine the Capacity of Business*

1. Maintaining positive attitudes, no matter what the market is doing.
2. Encouraging new experiences in the industry, trying new things, being different.
3. Taking control of your business, don't let it control you.
4. Understanding the customers, what they need, how you can impress them with your skill and services.
5. Being single minded in your purpose and your vision.
6. Getting in front of change in your office not behind it.

The revolutionary factors that change your business are driven by these values. They are brought to fulfillment by single-minded purpose and focus. Constant never-ending contact with your clients/customers reinforces your care and concern for them. Your value is reinforced by the use of your services. **Values are Powerful Lessons in Personal and Professional Change**

1.  Ethics are a cornerstone of influence. You cannot influence anyone without the projection of a strong personal image. No matter what the situation might be, integrity cannot be compromised.

2.  Focus on communication. The more focused your message, the deeper the impact of the impression and the more likely your profile in the community will increase.

3.  Balance. A business person has at the same time commitment to three marriages; spouse, work, community. The centre of the community will always achieve influence. When your life has balance, it will have meaning to you.

4.  Associate only with nurturing people. Birds of a feather flock together. You will be judged by the company you keep.

5.  Organize your time to be congruent with your values in order to attain personal happiness. How much of your personal life is really compatible with what you want to accomplish?

6.  What are you afraid to attempt? This block, once removed, will became your stepping stone to greatness.

7.  If you had only six months to live, how would that change your life?

8.  Rewrite your major goals once a day, or look at your goals at least four times a day. This will keep you moving forward through the obstacles. Visualize the ideal outcome.

MEET THE ENTREPRENEURS

*Meet the entrepreneur:* she is about five foot five, an elegant black woman.

As a child she was molested several times, as a teenager raped, as an adult violated. She came from the slums of Harlem. Today she is one of the highest paid women in the world. Did she marry wealth? No! Did she compromise herself and her integrity to climb the corporate ladder on the backs of men that were less talented? No! Did Aunt Matilda die and leave her a fortune? No! Her name is Oprah Winfrey; black, impoverished, female, minority. Her average yearly income today exceeds ninety million dollars. You ask if there is justice? I say, "Yes, here is an example."

*Meet the entrepreneur:* he is about five feet eleven inches.

He desperately wanted to be a healer in his country of India. In frustration about the lack of medical supplies, aid, and equipment in his impoverished land, he came to the USA as a medical doctor. Today, he gives lectures, writes books, and is paid over $65,000 for a one hour talk. He is Indian, minority, male, non-English speaking (initially). He is  called the guru of health. His name is Deepak Chopra. You ask if there is justice? I say, "Yes, here is an example."

*Meet the entrepreneur:* he is over six feet tall. Born in Jackson Point, Ontario, Canada.

In 1985, he was playing small clubs and university campuses as a standup comedian. He lived in a Volkswagen bus because he could not afford hotels on the road. Five years ago, he wrote himself a check for ten million dollars and put it into his pocket as a dream. Today, he earns twenty million dollars for each film, approximately three-to-four months of work. His name is Jim Carey. You ask if there is justice? I say, "Yes, here is an example."

**_Meet the entrepreneur:_** he is approximately six feet seven inches tall.

Some would say that his height would make him incapable of much except basketball. As a child, his father left the family in ruins. As a teenager he was taunted for his size.

The dinner at Thanksgiving was donated . He was a millionaire before the age of thirty. Today his yearly income exceeds one hundred and ten million dollars.

He is paid one hundred and twenty five thousand per talk. He is coach to athletes, presidents and royalty. His name is Anthony Robbins. You ask is there justice? I say, "Yes, here is an example."

> "Man is not the creature of circumstance; circumstances are the creatures of men."
>
> *Benjamin Disraeli*

Are you allowing circumstances or your past to dictate what you want out of life? The past does not predict the future unless you decide it shall. Decisions about who we are, who we spend time with, how we earn our living, all shape our destiny. Anthony Robbins writes, *"Decision making is the ultimate power; it allows you to engage the gifts that God has given you; to utilize all of your resources to create a greater quality of life—not only for yourself, but for all those you have an opportunity to touch."*

Strategies for success come not only from belief, they come from the heart. It is the heart energy that gives you the courage to step out of your comfort zones to accomplish feats of seeming impossibility to the rest of the world. If your heart energy is engaged in meaningful work . . . nothing can stop you. You literally become immortal in thought and deed.

The greatest people in history had heart energy engaged in their work. Nothing and no one stopped them. No one stopped Alexander Graham Bell from inventing the telephone, the Wright brothers from inventing the airplane, Ford from bringing the industrial revolution to an agricultural society, Bill Gates from bringing the computer age to an industrial society, John. F. Kennedy for believing in the space program or Dave Liniger from becoming the cowboy of the Internet. No one believed there would be a man on the moon. In 1969 this was also accomplished.

Strategies for the entrepreneur do not just come from great genes, great parents, great funding, great strategies or underlying plans for success. They come from every nerve, fiber, and sinew inside that cries, "I will go on!", when the rest of the world laughs and calls you crazy.

If we are to excel in any industry, we must ask ourselves if we are publicly perceived as being entrepreneurs?

### *What are the true characteristics of professionals?*

1.  What makes sports personalities outstanding?
    What did it cost them to be professional?
    How much time did they spend practicing?
2.  What are the values that drive the professional?
    Are their values meaningful to business?
3.  Have you asked yourself
    *   What is your passion?
    *   Does it lie in serving?
    *   Does it lie in your commitment?
    *   Does it lie in your soul's need to be the best?

Are you striving for excellence in your daily opportunity for full human potential? We can empower ourselves by being proactive in activities that have proven to work for others and incorporate these activities into our daily lives so that we live in our truth.

When we are so busy improving our lives, we have no time for negative actions or responses. We take the responsibility for our own lives in becoming shining stars within the community.

Change always happens from the inside out, not from the outside in. I can use my chosen path, my chosen field of accomplishments and dreams to be led forward. I can choose new beginnings in examination of myself and my business plans to be in alignment with my whole purpose.

We are created with the possibilities for miracles in our daily lives—let's learn to live them.

I was in my fourth year as a Realtor when I heard Brian Tracey talk about writing down goals. I didn't quite believe him when he said, "Just write down your goal, and it will magically happen." Since I worked in the top real-estate office in the province at that time my goal was to be #1 in that office as well as in the province.

Although I stopped paying attention to the goal and concentrated on my business, I was still startled 30 days later as I opened the newspaper and found a full page ad honoring me as the top agent in the company. This small trick still works today. It was always my goal to achieve two million dollar status in our office of very top producers at Re/max. I accomplished that this January—as well as writing two new books!

You cannot reach a goal as easily if your body, mind and spirit are not in harmony with the goal. When you find harmony within yourself, nothing will stop you once you set plans for your own success. The right people show up, the right money shows up, the right circumstance shows up.

Time will become an illusion because time stands still for the one in love.

When you plan your work and work your plan you will never be adrift on the ocean of opportunity because people will seek you out. Writing your business plan is the step by step roadmap to success. It will take you from rags to riches, provided you love what you do and are contributing to the community.

Work from the dream backwards. Work from the end result backwards to get to where you want to be tomorrow. When you decide you want to be the best, believe it will happen. Put it out to the universe to accomplish this goal, visualize the end result and your reality will find you.

Plan your vacation first. The greatest reward comes from enjoying the ski trip to Europe, the scuba diving or wherever the location of your dreams take you.

The only thing that counts is the quality of your life right now!

Envision your business as you want it to be. What does it look like, now?

1.  Name the activities that cause things to happen.
    What would occur if you doubled the intensity or the time it takes to do them? Would the profits in your business double?
2.  What are the commitments and promises that I must make to myself and others to create the vision?

A house is always built twice; once on paper in the blueprints, once with hammer, nails, mortar, brick. Unless you see clearly the vision of your dream business, you cannot achieve it unless you take steps to execute the plans.

Visualize first making it happen, then create your dream in actuality with passion, creativity, energy. Give your whole self. Don't hold back. Use the hammer of intentions:

- the nails of focus
- the mortar or glue of integrity
- the energy of your heart and your soul.

*The entrepreneur builds the empire in spirit, harmony and unity to reach financial immortality.*

# Chapter Three

# WIN!

## *What's Important Now?*

*I*t's the top of the sixth, the Cleveland Indians against the Boston White Sox. Cleveland pulls their pitcher because they're down five runs. Black Jack McDowell walks onto the mound amidst boo's. "Go home, you can't change this," is the general feeling in the stadium.

With bases loaded, Black Jack shut out the inning. Then he shut out the next inning and the next until he shut down the Boston White Sox. In the next four innings the Indians came from behind to win the game 11 to 5.

Black Jack walked off the mound to a standing ovation from 40,000 raving fans. There were no more boo's that day. There will be no more boo's because Black Jack understood the theory of "what's important now".

In order to win the game, he had to score a shut out. There were no other options.

I have played baseball with RE/MAX™ for the last seven years. Fortunately, I've always been on the winning team. Several years ago we played in tournament against some very tough competition. It was a sunny day and we started to play early in the morning. I only play the position of catcher because it keeps me in the game all the time.

Because it was such a beautiful day, I did not wear my cage to protect my face. I didn't expect the play to be rough so early in the morning. A few innings into the game, a pop fly went up right in front of me. As I turned to catch it, the sun caught my eye and instead of the ball landing in my glove, it landed in my eye. From ten feet up, it was a whopper of an impact.

The coach, Wally, yelled, "You won't be in the game with that eye any more."

I responded, "Let's see what's wrong before you decide that for me, thanks."

My eye was out three inches by the time I reached the dugout and I went straight to emergency from there, ice packs and all.

I made the decision that if there were no bones broken, and there was no damage to my eye, I would go back in. Well, there were no bones broken, and they told me that I would not know for six weeks whether or not my retina would detach. We couldn't wait six weeks, the final game was today.

There were no other options. "What's important, now?" I thought.

When I went back to the game with a bandaged eye under my cage, my winning team was down by six runs. I couldn't stand the tension. If your team was disqualified after the first round, they went to consolation, not to the finals. We worked hard that year to win it all, not just to settle for the consolation prize.

I told the coach to put me in for one inning and that I would take full responsibility for my eye. After much persuasion, he finally agreed.

When the team saw me behind the plate, cage, bandage and all, they understood the meaning of WIN. Within that one inning, they pulled out of nowhere ten runs. We finished the game five runs ahead. The boys laughed at the whopper of a shiner I sported for a week.

I played only one inning and had a runner run for me, but just the sight of a wounded player behind the plate was enough to make my team understand "what was important now". In the crunch, it's always the right time to do the right thing.

The movie *Liar, Liar,* is an example of a man so caught up in his legal practice, he constantly misses quality time with his son. In desperation, his ex-wife finally has enough and moves to another city with a man she's not in love with, but that she feels will prove a better father for her child than his biological father.

There are hilariously funny scenes of Jim Carey stealing a flight of stairs to run beside the plane, flagging down the plane to retrieve both his son and his ex-wife; tears streaming down his face.

In the crunch, his fabulous legal career was forgotten for something much more important; his family. He had no other options or he would lose them both.

Have you ever watched someone you love die? In the final moments of life on earth before the spirit leaves the body, does that person say to his beloved, "Show me the money?"

No. Generally he says to everyone he is leaving behind, "I love you."

"What's important now," means relationship. When there is no relationship, nothing will be important, nothing will matter. Where there is a relationship, it all matters, every small insignificant thing that you do or say. Every small insignificant thing that you don't do or don't say also matters.

Sins of omission are far more prominent than sins of error. Whether the relationship is that of customer or client to salesperson, that of salesperson to corporation, that of corporation to the environment, that of environment to society, that of society to universe. In the final analysis, before we draw our last breath, everything boils down to relationship.

"What's important now" means deciding where you are in the relationship. Are you making a commitment to go to the wall for that person, or are you asking them to "show you the money" so that you can find meaning in the paltry existence you call your life?

If your heart's not in it—get out fast! It will kill you if you don't. Work means love, and if you don't do what you love, find time for those you love. Display your love and say you love them or you have no hope of a WIN.

Life is always full for those who love. Time stands still for those who love.

The question of not having enough, being enough, doing enough just never comes up. They are too busy doing what they love, being with those they love and life is joyful and complete. There is always enough!

The issue of not having enough clients never comes up, because when you are heart to heart with your clients you go to the wall for them, don't they feel it? Don't you think they understand your pain in making the deal work or finding the solution to their problem? Don't you believe love is returned? How does that love manifest?

In the final analysis, don't all the greats in any career pick themselves up, out of the dirt and the mud to keep on slugging no matter what? The champions always know what it takes to WIN. They keep getting up. Is it ever "just for the money?" Or is it because, they have come heart beat to heart beat with someone they can love. Someone they can make a difference for, someone who's life they can change by being who they are? Living their almighty purpose before God and the world, they become important. We all sell someone something every day of our lives.

Before you do anything else in your career, decide to be heart beat to heart beat with the people that you serve. All else will fall into place. Eventually the money does show up, because the motives were right from the beginning.

Relationships make you REAL.

They are the only WIN you will ever need.

# Prologue

## Wizards, Myths, Fables, and Other Misnomers in Business

Dorothy traveled to Oz to meet the wizard. She wanted adventure in her life. This amazing man had the capacity to change any situation and change it for the good. The Tin man wanted a heart, the Lion wanted courage, the Straw Man wanted a brain, but most of all Dorothy wanted to go back to Kansas to see her family. All these wonderful adventures could be had by going to visit the wizard and asking for his favor.

After many adventures on their journey, the traveling companions finally got to Oz. There they found the wizard. He had a big, booming voice and strange contraptions all around him. Lights whizzed and fizzed everywhere. It seemed magical and untouchable to meet this hugely important man.

Dorothy went up to the Wizard, terrified of the outcome. He might be angry at her. At that very moment, her little dog Toto ran behind to pull the curtain for this magical man. The lights, curtains and drama fell aside and the mystical wizard of Oz was just an ordinary person, a small man, embarrassed at being found out he was not one of the Greek gods, but an ordinary human being.

So it is in business, that we see the business of running a business as rather magical, mysterious, and untouchable. The CEO is as untouchable and scary as the wizard was. The corporation as strange and mysterious a land as the Land of Oz. Marketing or prospecting as dragons to be slain.

The myths of what can not be done in business out

number the possibilities of what can be done in business. As a child I remember my mother reading Grimms' fairy tales to me at bed time. I remember it being a very comforting time of the day, one where all my troubles were forgotten and I could be absorbed in the adventures of the fairy story or incredible tale of adventure and intrigue.

My father taught me the basics of business from the time I could read.

As an entrepreneur and in taking the risks of an entrepreneur, I learned early on, that business is not magical, mysterious or untouchable.

It follows certain guidelines, certain patterns, and sometimes has the elements of a game. Coaches certainly know everything there is to know about the field of human endeavor and what it takes to WIN!

In remembering all the lessons I've learned over many years in business, explaining business, its "Rules" or non-rules led me to write the stories in the context of fables, myths and misnomers. I hope that they bring you pleasure and give you understanding that the lessons have been learned in lifetimes, of fierce battles on the plains of Greece, overwhelming victories in times of King Arthur, and fables of olde.

The battles on the fields of Greece or the stories of the villagers in small towns, are no different than the battles on the field of corporate structure, or the small business man in his struggles for market share and local fame.

The misnomers have occurred because we believe we can't, before we believe we can. We accept the ordinary as our fate, rather than the extraordinary.

We believe in lives of poverty, before we believe in lives of abundance, generosity and goodness.

May this small sampling of fairy stories cause your eyes

to open rather than drift shut before bedtime. May this small collection of tales, give you the lessons that you need to slay the dragons in any market.

# Secret One

# ALWAYS
# FOLLOW THE DREAM
## *Joseph's Technicolour Dreamcoat*

As the youngest son of Jacob, Joseph was hated by his brothers and their wives because he was the favorite son. His brothers could not say one kind word to him because they hated him so much.

Joseph had a dream. When he told it to his brothers they hated him all the more.

He said, "We were binding sheaves in the field when suddenly my sheaf rose and stood upright, while your sheaves gathered around mine and bowed down to it."

His brothers asked, "Do you intend to reign over us? Will you actually rule over us?" And they hated him all the more because of his dream.

Then he had another dream, and he also made the mistake of sharing that with his brothers.

"Listen," he said, "I had another dream and this time the sun, the moon and eleven stars bowed down to me." At this time, his father rebuked him.

"What is it that you intend, here?" Will your family

actually bow down to you?"

His brothers were jealous of him and his father kept this in mind.

He told him, "Your brothers are grazing the flocks near Shechem. Go see if all is well with them." So Joseph took the magnificent dreamcoat that his father had made for him and went to see his brothers.

Before he reached them, his brothers plotted to kill him.

"Here comes the dreamer," they said. "Come now let us kill him and throw him into the well where a ferocious animal may eat him. Then we will see what comes of his dreams."

When Reuben heard this he tried to rescue him from their hands. "Instead of killing him, why don't we sell him to the Ishmalites that are on their way to Egypt?"

Judah said, "What will we gain if we have our brother's blood on our own hands, let us sell him instead to the merchants and we will be rid of him."

The brothers returning to their land took Joseph's beautiful, technicolour dreamcoat and dipped it in the blood of a goat. When their father saw it, he put on sack cloth and mourned for the loss of his son.

The merchants in the meantime, sold Joseph again to Potiphar, captain of the guard of the Pharaoh. Joseph, in the house of the Egyptian master prospered the house. Everything that had been put in his care blossomed and grew.

The master withheld nothing from him and Joseph led a charmed life. One day Potiphar's wife desired him. Joseph refused her charms.

"How could I do such a thing and sin against my master and God?" he asked her. She caught him by his cloak and ran out of the house.

With that she had enough evidence to incriminate him. When his master heard the story, he threw Joseph into prison.

Again God showed Joseph favour and sometime later, Joseph was called upon to clarify the dreams of the Pharaoh officials. The events passed exactly as Joseph had explained.

Two years passed, Pharaoh had a dream. The chief cupbearer remembered Joseph's correct interpretation of his own dream and Joseph was sent to interpret the dream.

The Pharaoh said to Joseph, "In my dream I was standing in the Nile when out of the river came seven fat cows and they grazed among the reeds. After them came seven lean cows, scrawny and ugly. The seven fat cows ate up the seven lean cows.

In my next dream I also saw seven heads of grain growing on a stalk. After them seven other heads sprouted, withered, thin and scorched by the east wind. The seven thin heads also swallowed up the fat heads. I told this to the magicians, but no one could explain it to me."

Joseph said to the Pharaoh, "The dreams are the same. The land will experience seven years of plenty, followed by seven years of famine. The abundance in the land will not be remembered because of the famine that will ravage the land, it will be so severe.

The reason that the Pharaoh was given the dream in two forms is that the matter has been firmly decided and it will be done soon." With this, Joseph was put in charge of the land and the land prospered under him. The food was held in reserve and Egypt had plenty. As a result of his wisdom, Joseph was given the Pharaoh's ring and the position of being second in command in the land.

After seven years the country did experience famine. Joseph began to sell his grain to the neighboring countries that had not saved wheat during the harvest. All the countries came to buy grain from Joseph because the famine was severe in all the lands—except Egypt.

Jacob then sent his remaining ten sons to Egypt to buy grain. Although Joseph did recognize his brothers, they did not recognize him. They bowed before him in a request to buy food for the family.

Joseph wanted to test them and accused them of being spies. He put a silver cup in the grain with the sack of the youngest brother. When the servants discovered the cup, Joseph had the brothers sent before him.

As they threw themselves at his feet to beg for forgiveness, Joseph finally revealed "who" he was. He wept so loudly, that the Egyptians heard him outside the hall. His brothers were terrified. They could not answer him.

They were afraid that he would kill them for the injustice that they had committed against Joseph.

Joseph forgave them and gave them property for all of their household.

Jealousy and hatred are qualities that cause turmoil in all situations. They are a fact of life, as competition is a fact of business. Joseph had extraordinary visionary powers and was despised because he was different. He spent years in prison accepting the wrath of his family and finally reached a position of power, because he did not fight back. In the final analysis, he saved the lives of his family members because of his vision and extraordinary skills, and forgave them for their cruelty. These unusual qualities made Joseph unique as well as being a wise ruler.

Most entrepreneurs and companies succeed, not because they are the same as everyone else, give the same service, employ the same marketing techniques, but because they are different, unusual and unique. Those very qualities seek to enhance rather than detract from moving business forward towards success.

One of the major points of this book is that uniqueness and unusual vision are actually necessary in creating magical results in business.

It was the liberation of Joseph's talent as a dreamaker that caused him and his nation greatness. Over a period of many years of both wonderful times and hardship, Joseph established himself as a dreamaker. Because of Joseph's underlying need to make a meaningful contribution to society and to show extraordinary skill in shaping the destinies of the lives that he touched, as difficult as that was in prison, he continued to hold the vision of the dream in the most unfortunate circumstances. Without following the obstacles around the dreams over the hardship, through the rejection to final fruition of the vision, no glory is found.

We are as a people imprisoned by fears, past failures and by living in the past.

The dreamakers don't just live for today, their work, purpose, vision and mission takes them well into tomorrow and beyond. Whatever your dream is, continue to follow it from today until it materializes into abundance. Good fruits and great harvests are the results of happy dreamaking from now until forever.

# YOU ARE PERFECT
## *The Fable of The Tortoise and The Eagle*

*O*nce upon a time there was a tortoise, who desperately wanted to fly. He was tired of his lowly life on the ground and wanted to be an eagle. "If I could only get up into the air, I could soar with the best of them," he believed.

One day as the tortoise was sunning himself on a rock in the ocean, an eagle landed beside him.

"Oh, greatest of all the birds of the air," he begged, "please teach me how to fly so that I may be as graceful as you." He offered him all the treasures in the sea, if only the eagle would teach him to be an eagle rather than himself.

At first the eagle declined because he knew that not only was this situation absurd, it was also impossible. After being begged and begged, he finally agreed.

The eagle took the tortoise to great heights. Without any lessons closer to the ground, the tortoise had not discovered that flying would not give him as much joy and freedom as he believed.

Once he had reached past the clouds, the eagle loosened

his hold and asked the tortoise to fly if he could. Before the tortoise could express any thanks, he fell upon a huge rock and was dashed to pieces.

One of the great lessons of life is to enjoy being "who" you are. We were not all born to be eagles or born to be tortoises. Rather than trying to be who you are not, concentrate on being who you are. You were given unique gifts. Enhance those gifts every day to bring miracles into your life. Don't try to be someone else.

The hungry state of passionate expectation and internal certainty of success are the key ingredients to personal victory in who we are today and the destiny that we intend to carve out tomorrow. Victory does not show up in trying to become someone else. Victory shows up in making the choices that enhance the levels of performance at what we do best as ourselves and by our unique, perfect nature. We were created perfect—just enough as we are. Thank goodness they broke the mold when you were born! Your genius in your capacity is enough!

At the end of the day as we all stand before St. Peter at the pearly gates the question will be, "How much of your potential did you use?"

"How much of your potential did you leave untapped?"

Releasing our own potential for greatness lies within the individual and within the collective company or corporation. Contributing to excellence, transforms every interaction and captures the magic of our very existence.

*Secret Three*

# PASSION IS NOT A FOUR LETTER WORD. . .FEAR IS!

*The Parable of The Crow
and The Two Seeds*

*I*n the world we live in today, the pace of our lives, the chemicals (drugs, alcohol or food) that we ingest, the lifestyle that we choose can numb us to the passions of life. We feel naked and rather insecure about moving forward towards success and embracing all those scary emotions that come along with the feelings of change. We, therefore, delay the appreciation of our own good. In stifling passion or numbing life purpose, we invite the sinister monster of fear to come visit us and sit by our side haunting our every move lest we make another mistake. We accept our good without even looking for our better.

Fear of course, like a dragon or a snake, envelopes us in it's clutches and by keeping us wrapped in it's own arms immobilizes us. Fear of beginnings, just like fear of endings, debilitates us and drives us deeper into the rut of boredom and sameness. If you always do what you've always done, you always get what you always got—we all know the truth of that statement. Yet, the sinister monster of fear keeps us imprisoned in our sameness, in boredom.

When we resist the energy of the universe or our soul, pointing the way to greatness in our lives, we experience shaky out of control feelings. These feelings of not being in control scare us. Truth is expressed in accepting these shaky feelings, feelings of insecurity or vulnerability as a sign that we are on the right track.

Are travesties or tragedies placed in our path to illuminate our power, or to diminish it? Isn't that our greatest fear? In his 1994 inaugural speech, Nelson Mandela summed this up very well:

"Our deepest fear is not that we are inadequate,

Our deepest fear is that we are powerful beyond measure.

It is our light, not our darkness that frightens us most.

We ask ourselves, 'Who am I to be brilliant, gorgeous or talented or famous?'

Actually, who are you not to be?

You are a child of God.

Playing small doesn't serve the world.

There is nothing enlightened about shrinking

so that others won't feel insecure around you.

As we let our light shine, we unconsciously give other people permission to do the same.

As we are liberated from our own fear,

Our presence automatically liberates others."

Complacency causes a deeper rut than the tomb. We begin to live our lives in tomb or womb-like envelopment of complacency, sameness and fear of change. As we are imprisoned we are doomed to the lives of our parents, grandparents, or forefathers should we choose not to change. We accept their fate and destiny without challenge.

Although the world rotates forward on it's axis daily, people don't seem to think that they should move forward with change on their axis. Experiencing new things, eating new foods, visiting new places all enrich us and our capacity for experience in the human form as an enhancement, an enlargement. Ultimately until we find our purpose and life passion we don't really move forward, experience life force energy or zest. Breaking free from the constrictions and restrictions that bind us with or without our knowledge or permission is cited as unusual for most western culture.

Because it is uncomfortable to change, we don't. Because complacency, the womb, or the tomb, no matter how you look at it is comfortable, we stay there. When disaster is threatening our lives or our businesses, and change becomes mandatory through outside forces, rather than those inside, we finally take up the gauntlet to create change. Even when business is booming, and we need to hire more staff, change location, change our outlook, change our business plan, it still creates discomfort. Risk is a factor we don't like to embrace—it might change who we are. We may even succeed, if we change. Scary thought.

Authors get to do fun activities when they're not walking around with either a computer or a phone as a permanent attachment to their bodies. When you need an intellectual breakthrough, the best remedy is a physical breakthrough, that is to do a physical activity. So, in the preparation for this book, I took the plunge, quite literally, stepping out of my comfort zones as an athlete desiring a change in my capabilities as a skier, and went to ski school at Mont Tremblant, Quebec.

I went inspired to learn this seemingly mysterious sport and ended up with a class of other more terrified never-

never skiers than I was. In two days, I went from terrified beginner to lusting for more speed at every turn at every hill. Our instructor, Claudia, led us through terror barrier after terror barrier. As day three approached we were actually not seizing up in fear at the thought of taking on the intermediate runs. Claudia constantly asked, "Are you ready?" I knew I was in the right place at the right time. That question became my question.

We moved forward through our fears. At one point she said, "Angie, follow me." Like lemmings to the sea, we all followed. Although the hill had a blind corner, none of us took off our boots and said that we were going home when the other side of the slope turned into a sheer drop of nothingness. There was a point of no return. Either this mountain was going to conquer us or we were going to conquer it.

Somehow at the bottom of the hill, we all arrived and had all survived, even if it required more than one intimate experience with the snow. No one laughed at the attempts to conquer the mountain, we all cheered the survivors at the bottom. Interestingly enough, each one on my team moved from fear into passion in that exercise. The greater the terror, the greater the fear, the greater the passion. It's getting to the other side of the fear that counts. Passion waits there.

There were many lessons in that ski week, the skill of learning to ski became a secondary by-product. Learning about conquering the mountain and my fears are lessons to keep for the end of time. The mountain wins when you stop your momentum, when you stop making the turns, when you reduce the speed or the rhythm because of fear.

Yet continuing to make the turns, no matter how steep the hill, or continuing to keep the rhythm of the gait, the mountain seemed to know that you were serious about this. He let you win. The feeling of winning over fear is glory!

The universe bows to do our bidding when we step from fear into passion and continue to move forward through our terror barriers. No complacency here, pushing always faster to be in the harmony of the forward movements, harmony with control . . . stretching for the finish.

The world of business is no different. The fable of the crow and the two seeds is a lasting illustration of this point.

## THE FABLE OF THE CROW AND THE TWO SEEDS

Once upon a time there were two seeds that were dropped into the soil by a farmer planting in the early spring. The first seed found the ground cold and uninviting. Rather than boring a deep nest for himself in the ground, he decided to lay there until an opportunity for warmth and comfort presented itself to him.

His friend, the second seed, also found the ground cold and uninviting, but decided to dig himself a warm bed in the spring soils, perhaps the soils would warm up once he was safe inside. Although this new environment was not comfortable, he dug down deep, sent his shoots into the soil, stabilized his position, eventually warmed up and started to grow.

At the very moment that the seeds were deciding their fate, a crow was passing by overhead. The seed that had dug a home for himself and was content to grow, of course could not be seen. The seed that lay on the top complaining how life had been so cruel to him, refusing to accept the risk of growth, was quickly gobbled up as a tasty morsel for the crow.

The moral of the story is: it is better to risk discomfort,

stretching forward in your ventures, than to wait for the ideal conditions that may never present themselves.

Opportunities for growth happen when you know nothing will stop you from your dreams and passions.

Rather than waiting to be comfortable, we challenge ourselves when we move forward out of our fears and into our passions. In seeking the challenge growth occurs, and fear disappears. Passion awaits with a smile.

# TIME IS OF THE ESSENCE
## *The Fable of the White Rabbit*

*T*he fable of the White Rabbit is one that we are all familiar with in the children's story of Alice in Wonderland. The White Rabbit runs all over the story sporting a pocket watch and constantly complaining about not having enough time. His battle cry is, "I'm late, I'm late for an important date!" Don't we all feel that from time to time?

Some of us feel that day to day. Some of us feel that hour to hour, or even minute to minute. The interesting point is that although the White Rabbit complains about never having enough time, he squanders what he does have in complaints.

Time management is not only a cornerstone to good business, it is a cornerstone to good living. We cannot live a life without those we love around us, yet we frequently confuse issues of urgency with issues of importance. To assume responsibility for a great business, begin with WIN . . . WHAT'S IMPORTANT NOW.

Let the rest of the world revolve around that one issue.

Get the tasks that are important done first. Look at tasks that are urgent by their demands or by their nature and schedule them around the important tasks.

I could write volumes on the issue of time management alone. I am asked at least three times a week how I get so much done, in so little time with so little effort.

For myself and my company I hold the vision of the future, for all the people that my company currently employs or will employ. As much as I hold myself responsible for my own achievement, I am also held responsible for the achievement of others my work touches. Daily, I remind myself of the vision of building an empire that is safe, secure, stable within and gives us financial freedom and time freedom. There is no time freedom without financial freedom, relationship freedom and genius freedom.

In order to get all the things done that need to be done in a day, we need to be present and in the moment with all relevant tasks. Especially with relevant people.

Einstein was a brilliant man. When he created the Theory of Relativity, he gave us a business theory based on the principle of energy. In juggling issues, timetables and schedules remember energy.

When you begin to live your life with $E=MC^2$ everything falls into place. This theory remembers that energy is equal to the mind consciousness that surrounds it to the power of two. Two people in the same consciousness have the power of eleven—that's the power of masterminding.

You're probably asking, what is she talking about? I'm talking about choices. The choices you make every minute of every hour of every day. Whether consciously or subconsciously, we make choices that propel us forward or hold us back. These choices are found in the energy of the company we keep, the type of clients we choose to work with or who choose to work with us, and in the levels of integrity we have in our interactions with everyone we relate with. It is the theory of relativity, remember. All things are relative to energy.

I know I am energized by people with similar thinking to mine. I know I am energized by friends that believe in me and support my writing and speaking. I know I am energized by inspirational films, seminars, or music. By my nature I am a very introverted person.

It's all a matter of internal energy. I move forward. My energy is reserved for forward momentum only.

Heart energy, and mind energy is on the completion of our next tasks to propel our company forward. It's just that simple. In the final analysis, all complex issues of time management really chunk down to the basic question, "Does this conversation or this task move me toward or away from my goal or my purpose? If the answer is away from, get moving to the next person, conversation or task that will bring you closer to the energy of your goals.

Again this requires conscious choices. Who can spend time with on a quality basis that will bring the goal to me? Who can I help that will rave about my services to bring the goal to me? Who can I serve that will bring the goal to me?

Start first, to look at your time frames of expectation. When I sold real estate, I looked at my expenses for each month. I took this goal and the expectation of myself to achieve this goal and decided, it would not take me a month to accomplish meeting expenses. I would take a week. After I had met the goal, everything from that point on would be profit. I named this point, point zero. Until I was profitable, I was at zero. Could you live a whole life at point zero? Yes,

I've seen many of my friends do it!

From that point my life was organized around this goal. Who should I call on to reach the goal? How many clients would it take to sell one million dollars worth? Two million? How many deals, at what percentage, in what time frame did I need to accomplish what I wanted?

I sold real-estate and wrote books at the same time, for four years. The two activities are not in the same head space at all. It got to be a real time management dilemma. How many clients did I need so I could take three days off real estate to write? How many clients did I need to take vacations so I could experience more, to write more?

How many calls did I need to make to have those clients? If I made those calls, how many real clients would I have as a result? I never lost sight of the goals, or the relationship with my family and friends that supported all of it. Ultimately that is why we work isn't it? To provide a better way of life for our family isn't it?

The question of time management is the core issues of our existence. I needed to find a way to live my dream without giving up my income or being accused of abandoning my family, I had to learn how to schedule "what's important," first.

The Swiss cheese method always works—just as Swiss cheese is full of holes, so you should leave room in your work for gaps or holes of completion. When you look at a picture, the frame is also a part of the picture. When you look at a page, the spaces around the page are also part of the page. Just like the holes are a part of the cheese, so the gaps are necessary in your work.

Albert Camus once said, "Real generosity toward the future consists in giving all the the present."

Instead of seeing the need for completion, gaps on the

page act to enhance the page and make it interesting. The gaps in the calendar indicating your holidays should be completed first, making your life interesting. The gaps in your day should be filled in first with the important, then with the urgent, and all the details in between. Just as the gaps in the cheese make the cheese authentic—so the gaps in the pages of your life make your life authentic.

The most important criteria here is to do a reverse timeline for completion, filling in the tasks from the end result back to the beginning, thereby chunking down the small jobs that are needed to finish the work on the due date. Budgets adhering to the completion date become an integral part of the project, as do the people you need and their creative thinking.

If the task or project is not flowing smoothly along, learn to go with the flow and do something else instead. For whatever reason you run into an obstacle, give the obstacle the honor it requires by acknowledging it and quickly moving on to something else that is less challenging and easier for you, but still adds to the goal. We always think the most difficult jobs should be handled all at once instead of a bit at the time. Rather than wasting your energy in complaints like the White Rabbit, become proactive with the tasks you can do to finish this goal.

How do you chew an elephant? One bite at a time.

We have a huge calendar in our office with deadline dates for book publishing, speaking engagements and conferences. The team is aware of the tasks necessary for getting the show on the road and the dates of each deadline.

I just love that calendar. It keeps everyone on track and on purpose without my saying a word. It clearly indicates time off and time to work.

Neither my creative energy while writing, nor my

audience energy while speaking, needs to be cluttered by details that belong to the team. Once I get overloaded with details, I fragment. Fragmenting as a human is very much like a computer on overload which fragments the material it has in the hard drive. You know the information is there, you just can't access it in an intelligent manner.

My traveling time on airplanes or trains is used to write or to research for the next book or public talk. While I am away, the team handles the phone calls, the follow-up, the letters, the mass mailings, the ordering, the follow up on accounts, the operations, so I am free to be "on purpose" for the audience that has hired me to uplift them. My job is to inspire those people with passion for being. The neat byproduct of this is that the audience energy is greater than my energy. WIN! WIN!

Off-time is spent with those I love and who love me— complete attention to them is all I'm interested in. Again WIN! WIN ! I take the time to be totally present with every interaction whether on the phone or in person. Friendship is always easy. In today's fast pace intimacy is the challenge with those we love.

Just as you get past the layers of small talk in a friendship, it is important to get past the layers of unnecessary tasks that you should delegate to do real volumes of business.

There is no point in carving out a living, if you neglect to carve out a life.

# THE PAIN-BRINGS-GAIN MYTH

*Inspiration Rather Than Perspiration—*
*Belling the Cat*

*O*nce upon a time a number of mice called a meeting to decide upon the best means of getting rid of a cat that had killed many of their family members.

Various plans were discussed and rejected, until at last a young mouse suggested that a bell be hung around the neck of the cat, so in future they would have warning of the cat's movements and be able to escape her claws.

The suggestion was received joyfully by all, except an old mouse, who sat silent for a long time then got up and said, "While I consider this to be an inspired plan, and feel it would prove very successful if carried out, I should like to know who is going to place the bell on the cat? Who will bear the pain of the cat catching him, should he fail?"

This wonderful illustration again by Aesop, captures the essence of the pain brings gain myth. The mice felt in order to eliminate their constant pain from the enemy, they would devise a plan.

Although belling the cat was an inspired idea, there were

painful consequences, should the plan fail. The number one key to wealth is to learn to write out your goals in the form of a question. The more outrageous the answers, the more talented and brilliant the results will be.

Mindstorm twenty answers to your problem. Don't stop until you get twenty. Throwing your whole self into gear you will find solutions you were not expecting.

Excellence is found in the belief and expectation that the universe will give you anything that you ask of it, given that you ask often enough and creatively enough.

In getting on with your goals in the next year, put them on paper in the present tense as though you have already achieved them. Inspired moments will show up by accident.

In being excellent, we decide to pay a price in overcoming the obstacles that are standing in our way.

When you figure out why you are here and are led by your purpose, inspiration rather than perspiration will be the result. Your vision as your guide will attract the constructive steps required to accomplish whatever you desire.

The qualities of successful people make them unfailingly optimistic in every problem. Thinking in positive terms and with positive expectations brings solutions to seemingly impossible tasks. The impossible can be handled immediately, miracles take a little longer.

Problems are never sent to give you perspiration. They are sent as a special gift to your capacity of inspiration and for your own growth. All that matters is your interpretation and attitude while in the problem. Thinking about the future gets you there dulling the pain of previous failures with new found belief.

There does not need to be pain in your life to provide gain to your business. When inspired enough, you will welcome obstacles encouraging your creativity and success.

# THE BUTTERFLY THEORY
## *Making the Market*
## *Work For You*

*I*magine it's a beautiful spring day, and you decide to go for a walk or a run in the meadow of your life. As you finally sit on a log to look at the stream, you notice that a beautiful butterfly just landed on a clump of flowers at your feet. As you watch this gorgeous butterfly and examine it's beautiful details, it leaves the nectar of the flowers and lands on your shoulder. It is so beautiful and in your astonishment and amazement at what has happened, you suddenly turn, hoping to capture this gorgeous creature and keep it in a jar, keep it any way that you possibly can, but keep it you must.

In your haste, you turn suddenly, and the butterfly, sensing your immediacy, leaves. Your hopes are dashed for making this creature of the wild, your own. You follow it, pursue it, chasing for hours through the meadow. Everytime you get close, the butterfly, turns, flies off in a new direction, and you frantically chase again. Until, in your haste of capture, you fall over the log where you met the butterfly in the first place.

As you lie there in your disarray and discomposure, the butterfly notices and lands on your shoulder, yet again! The butterfly rests at your side, as you turn to grab it, disappears again.

This is the parable of the elusive market. Just like the butterfly, we barely have the right market in our grasp and poof, it's gone again. Market conditions change, world markets change, money markets change, the political arenas change, the bottom line changes as a result.

It's been my experience, that we are too shallow in our approach as to how many markets are at our disposal when we have a product or a service to offer. Sometimes we look only at the small nucleus of a geographic market, our own back yard, so to speak. This market could be as small as three square miles or it could be international—broader in scope than our imagination could ever be.

We could also have permutations of this market when we add the dimensions of other languages, other cultures. These permutations become greater when we again add a mix of:

- media
- print advertisement
- direct mail
- personal promotion through flyers
- telemarketing
- joint ventures
- radio, television, film, infomercials
- the Internet
- product on CD Rom, audio, video
- networking through client lists
- distribution channels, mass merchandising

In using some or all of these resources in our business plan, we also ensure a strong and steady market for our products and services. Planned diversity is the key.

In using at least two different forms of promotion and publicity, we reach the markets where we have the most to exchange. Marketing is exchange. I exchange my products and services for your products or services or money.

Basic, primitive, easy. The cave men did it just that way without money. Do we really need to reinvent the wheel?

So take the approach to your business that you are either a great inventor or a great scientist looking for a cure to an incurable disease. You already have the product, service, staff, location, and price. What other ingredients do you require in this amazing cure or invention?

You need the tools of marketing. Without marketing your business will lie dormant for years. You need only to discover two types of marketing styles that suit you and your business and then run with those. In discovering which market niche works for you, try a different one every other month until you see results.

Experimenting for more than a thirty days is too much when you're choosing your style.

But failing to implement at least two marketing niches, results in demise should the current conditions change. Change they will. Rather than panicking at the current market conditions, find another market, another medium to promote yourself in, and another geographic region to sell your products or services. Be like the butterfly and look for a new meadow. The butterfly is only being elusive, he has not disappeared out of your life forever.

If the current market is drying up, think of why? Could it be that you have only marketed in visualization, or only in audio, only in print, only on radio? Think about a new style of presentation, not changing the product, but only presenting it in a different medium. Think about something that you have used excessively, or not used at all to promote yourself. Then try that something new. Add at least two styles of marketing every other month to your current marketing approach and see if it makes a difference.

Remember the inventor. If this combination doesn't work take away one ingredient at a time to test the market. Test, test, and retest until you find the combinations that work. Very often these combinations are not what you are looking for, but remember, everyone thinks and perceives differently.

What makes your business boom may not be the same combination that someone else uses. Every business style is unique. Stay in harmony with yourself when trying something new. Ethics matter. Giving away your integrity is never the compromise.

Take away the marketing styles that don't work. Add different ones that do, increase the tempo, rate and number of those that do work. See what happens when you play a little game with yourself and your business. Small experiments are great. You don't need to break the bank.  Even a forty dollar ad in a paper you hadn't tried yet, could help. The secret is not to have any predetermined thoughts on the market that you believe might work, just try a few experiments and see what happens.

The combinations and permutations of marketing are different for every product, service and person. Although we don't enjoy telephone marketing, the results are so amazing, that we continue to do it. Should we rely solely on that medium for business, it would be tiring after a while. Therefore, at least two other medium must be used for maximum results.

The more I cater to the needs of the public for the mutual benefit of all parties, the more my business grows. Past clients, referrals, vertical markets are all places I turn to when there is a slump in the external market conditions. I say external market conditions because the market, whether booming or bust is still only in your head and in your personal experience. Another person on the same street with the identical market and identical product may be booming while your business is bust! He's found his market!

Vertical markets are found in geographic markets. All buildings that go up are considered vertical markets—all high rises, all office buildings, all towers where there is more than one business are vertical markets. My greatest years of success have been in the vertical markets of corporations. Do well for the CEO and everything else follows. Save the company money, make their employees happy, save time and presto! The butterfly of happiness lands on your shoulder and stays for a long time.

It's also physically easier to visit three markets in one building vertically than it is to travel three square miles by foot to cover the same number of people. Helping people get what they want, solving their problems should be your only focus. The secret is exchange. Solving their problems creates market niches for you. The more people you help, the more you get what you want—a market niche. Then, **get rich in your niche.**

The more often we work with current and past client lists and keep those people in our marketing plans, the more we become a household word. This rings especially true when someone who was a past client buys or sells something of yours with someone else because you were too busy to follow up. Then it's too late to pay attention. Learn to use these wake up signals to improve your business. Taking care of clients is your number one priority.

Although there are lots of fish in the sea, the real statistics are that it takes five times as much capital, resources, time to sell a new client as to resell an old one. Doesn't it make sense to have thousands of old clients and to keep reselling them and everyone that they know? Doesn't it make sense to work and rework those old client lists than to spend money trying to buy the business through expensive advertising only? Think profitability in time and money.

Follow up is always 95% of the business. Follow up until the cows come home. You'll have a better barn to put them in.

Learn to see opportunity where others see failure. Learn that finance is a creative process, and new ideas, styles or promotions are necessary for growth. Besides, it makes the business you're already good at enjoyable and fun. The only unhappy millionaires that I know are bored with their lives. Anyone contributing to society in a major way is happy working at what they do best. Time stands still when you love what you do.

Growing your business means growing yourself. It means consistently doing those things that make you money, and discarding or avoiding those things that don't work or hurt your bottom line. Where attention goes, money flows. Only pay attention to those parts of your business that consistently bring in profit. Discard those that cost too much in energy, time and money for the amount of return. You should be looking for a conservative return of 4:1 ratio. If I am prospecting daily, that return goes up to 90-95% of profitability.

When your focus becomes, 'how many people can I help today,' the how-to takes care of itself. Consistently seeking the marketing niches that your business thrives on and consistently discarding those that don't work for you, will give you the peace of mind to have the butterfly of happiness land on your shoulder—and stay. Your business will become a meadow of joy and opportunity.

# WALKING THE TIGHTROPE FINANCIALLY

## *Surfing the Networks*

We all love the circus. The fun, the popcorn, the cotton candy, the excitement, the death-defying feats of the tightrope walker, often without a net. If that person made one false move instant death would result. As scary and irrational as this dangerous act is in the circus, some of us think nothing of performing death-defying feats in our businesses and sometimes in our relationships.

I continue to validate this point because good business is just a series of successful relationships, one after another. The question is do we have the net in place before we start to walk across the tightrope? Do we put legs under the chair before we sit down?

As much as the tightrope walker has options to make his claim to fame more believable, such as practicing for years or using a net to break the fall should he make a mistake, we also have options to exercise in exploring the fields or sources of business. It is as critical to the long term success of our businesses to have the net in place before we begin the walk. This tightrope of financial suicide makes us much less vulnerable when we protect ourselves with options found in the "net."

At this point you're wondering how I know this?

It's called the circus of my own experiences. As a single mom raising four children I had to learn the secrets of business quickly.

I could not wait for the children to grow up. They needed food and shelter every day. I couldn't send them to the forest to follow the crumbs. Since I did not have millions of dollars to start my business, I had to learn to be smart with the bottom lines, protect myself from every fall for the very existence of my family was at stake every day.

Gender differences have nothing to do with financial success or opportunities. I could have chosen the easier route and gone to work in a less risky business than real estate, but the income was there for me even in the worst recession. It also gave me time flexibility to raise my family alone. There was never anyone demanding that I stay after five, and I could work from home on the systems to do research, while children were in bed. Eventually my children also became skilled at computers because they contributed to research on the computer. All are computer literate and speak three languages, it was great training for them at an early age.

Clarity of commitment to business accumulation is critical for yourself and others in the reality of your business. It is the essence of growth. Working every day on having huge numbers of people to contact and keeping these contacts alive and well is the net that will cushion your fall, if you ever have a change in the current market—and change it will.

Clearly define what it is that you are trying to

accomplish. Look at your service in terms of your market niche, then start to organize yourself with financing, research, marketing, personnel, computers and a sensible location to meet your objectives. Most business fail because of a lack of this business organization, and overestimating the current market. If you don't anticipate market changes, presto, you'll fall without a safety net waiting to catch you.

Let's look at possible places for the network that will ensure your success.

1. The geographic farm—they have to know you exist locally.
2. The sphere of influence—everyone you know in every group.
3. The corporate sphere—vertical markets are the greatest return for time
4. Current and past clients—help enough people you always have residual income.

The six month or yearly plan focuses your thinking in business terms. This is the way everybody does it. It never quite worked very well for me this way. If you are a sprinter, shorter goals are better for you. If you are a marathoner, you will keep your focus on the long term. I'm a sprinter. I decided to work on my objectives using a 90 day plan. There had to be an "x" number goals done in 90 days, or I had not met my objectives. Since I'm the CEO of my company, I had a very irate boss if the goals did not work out.—me.

To make the game even more fun, I would challenge myself to 30 day plans. Understand that you really have to get the lead out, when your goals are only 30 days long—anyone can be a superstar for 30 days—it takes real skill to do this repeatedly. The interesting point is that once you get cruising, and the momentum is right, you never have to look at your direction because your momentum takes care of the return on whatever investment you have made in your business. That means get your speed up and your business will always give you an equal exchange or better. Don't wait. Your profitability depends on it. Sometimes, just increasing the speed is enough to give you more profits.

Remember the skier on the hill. Maintaining the momentum and making a turn whenever there is an obstacle will keep you moving forward in the direction of the goal. The mountain will know that you are serious about this accomplishment and you get to win!!!!

Newton's law of gravity works in business as well as on gravity. An object in motion remains in motion. An object at rest remains at rest. The object in motion should be you. You should be contacting all the networks in order to keep your business in financial order, rather than walking the tightrope terrified of a fall.

So, let's look at your networks.

1. Family and friends
2. Business and trade organizations
3. Past jobs
4. Geographic zones—places in the neighborhood they know you.
5. Centers of influence
6. Clubs and community organizations.
7. Agencies and schools
8. Specific demographic areas according to age . . . Colleges to retirement homes
9. Corporations

Now let's look at how we contact these networks:

1. Direct mail—mass mailings
2. Telephone—.mass telephone calls
3. Flyers—follow up to telephone calls
4. Advertising—not the first priority
5. Door-knocking—no it's not old fashioned—
it still works!

These sources of income are not always fun to contact. No one said it was fun to do. The secret is *it* always generates income. When you train yourself to do the activities that daily cause you income—profit happens.

All spectacular success is preceded by unspectacular preparation.

You are not at work unless you are prospecting for the next client, while taking care of the one just sold. As you and your office commit to daily prospecting, the results of your income sources will go up exponentially. Combining different sources of networks with different types of prospecting and marketing will propel your business forward to superstardom.

Never again will you walk the tightropes financially when you surf the networks.

Don't forget the Internet is a current source of advertisement and information. In some fields, the Internet sites are still under construction. It is your job to tie up a site on the net with your name on it as soon as possible. The rumor mill has it that Nike paid ten million to get its site back from someone who had it before. Get yourself on the "NET" even if the purpose is only to send inexpensive e-mail to all your friends and family. It arrives instantly and costs less than pennies at a time.

After you have placed your contacts in a workable

database, learn to assess, re-evaluate and get going. As your business style changes and your contact sources are analyzed you will find yourself drawing more and more from certain sources. This is good. Follow the leads that make you money. Collect the rest into databanks so that it is available to you in the event that the market crashes or dries up. The networks concept must always give residual options to plan strategies that work with the information  me receive. Surfing the networks gives us pleasure in surfing and exploring every option in all situations.

Time is wasted when you are not organized in your current data bases and must redo all the tasks that are involved in daily, repetitive contact calls. I have found a minimum of 7 contacts a year will keep your databases healthy and happy. This keeps clients aware that you still exist and are interested in them. Should you decide to leave your current occupation, the data bases will serve you well somewhere else. If they do not you can sell them for profit and the next person can also profit from your effort rather than the energy of the work wasted and forgotten.

Redesign your networks to keep your closely aligned with your goals. Waste not, want not.

Keeping those databases handy always creates options for you when business is good and you are changing market strategy. When business is bad and you need to dig deep for instant profits, the data bases create gold.

### The Fifteen Commandments of Professional Growth
from Networking Success by Anne Boe

1. Thou shall have a sense of humor and be able to laugh at yourself, and with others when you make mistakes or errors.
2. Thou shall be responsible and accountable for your own

actions or lack of action, decision, behavior. Do not pass the blame.

3. Thou shall go the extra inch, mile, or light year that it takes to become successful and your own person.

4. Thou shall take chances, risks, and gambles or you will never realize any appreciable gain or growth.

5. Thou shall be a pro-active networker with high visibility.

6. Thou shall communicate effectively by listening to others, concentrating on facts, being receptive to learning and taking in bits of knowledge daily.

7. Thou shall have spunk, determination, never quitting before you've given it your best shot and then some.

8. Thou shall plan, prepare, and professionally present yourself to others in order to achieve proper placement.

9. Thou shall hone and polish your skills, competencies, and talents lest you become ineffective or stale.

10. Thou shall be a go getter. Be aggressive, assertive, ambitious. Attitude always determines altitude!

11. Thou shall work at what you love, love, love!

12. Thou shall be confident, reliable, and unconditionally co-operative and helpful to others. Humility and service precede praise and exultation.

13. Thou shall have no hidden agendas, anger, or resentment; play your cards face up, accept the truth.

14. Thou shall be kindly, candid, honest, truthful and diplomatic under all circumstances and under all existing conditions.

15. Thou shall be kind, generous, compassionate, understanding and patient. Be a valued friend!

Get out of yourself and into other people and watch your business flourish and grow.

Anne Boe, *Networking Success*

# PROMOTION IS COMMUNICATION
## *The Fable of the Fox and the Goat*

One day a fox fell into a well, and wondered how he would possibly get out again. At last a goat came along, feeling thirsty, he inquired of the fox, if the water was good. The fox wanted to promote his cause. Pretending he was swimming for pleasure, he replied, "Yes, come down my friend; the water is so good that I cannot get enough of it, and there is plenty for both of us."

The goat thinking that the fox meant the water was good for drinking, jumped in.

The fox making artful use of the goat's horns quickly sprang out.

Safely at the top of the well, he coolly remarked to the goat, "Had you thought first about yourself, you would have looked before you leaped. I'm glad that I convinced you of what you wanted. Thank you for helping me."

This wonderful tale from Aesop illustrates the simple principles of promotion.

Promotion is nothing more than communication with

another party to convince them, that your product is worth leaping for.

There is a powerful connection between our belief in ourselves and our work empowerment. We must be very bold and artful in our message to the community.

The magic begins in broadcasting:

| | |
|---|---|
| quality | leadership |
| service | honesty |
| greatness | professionalism |
| effectiveness | |

out to the community where it all begins. In order to accept this new challenge of making a bold difference, commitment, and contribution to our community we need to seek personal responsibility for where our business stands today and where we want to take it in the future.

Dramatic public promotions are the only way to go.

1. Rent a movie THEATRE to advertise your product and invite all your clients on a Saturday morning or matinee.
2. Go to a high school to talk about your product or service. There are always career days.
3. Run for fun . . . to raise money for the community. Have a community garage sale. Advertise or ask the local paper to cover the event.

4. Organize a golf day. Invite all your clients to play golf on you.
5. Lecture at a local fair/mall on your product or service, or have a kiosk in a local mall.
6. Write a community update newsletter at least once a quarter to inform your clients about what's new in your profession or your market.
7. Deliver 10,000 flyers in your neighborhood. Follow up with calls to inquire. When you follow up any mailing with a call, your client retention rate goes up by 30%.

8. Free evaluations in your product line at a fair, a mall, a neighborhood event. Remember your marketshare is always neighborhood oriented.
9. Radio and T.V. talk shows . . . volunteer to help. Promote your product on air. Public T.V. is free.
10. Any and all joint ventures you can think of with complimentary businesses in your neighborhood.

The bolder and more dramatic the promotion becomes the broader your market share will become. This works for any type of business in any type of market.

*Secret Nine*

# DIALING FOR DOLLARS
*Telephone Techniques for Profit*

*T*he telephone is the place that we make the biggest impression in business, no matter the reason is for our call. When you learn to use the telephone as your lowest cost, highest income producing investment tool, you will capture moments in your telephone conversations that are literally pure gold.

GUIDELINES TO SUCCESS ON THE TELEPHONE

*Incoming Calls:*

1. Smile! Believe it or not it shows in your voice. A happy disposition always reflects how interested you are in the client.
2. Focus only on the needs of the other party. They may be giving you critical information that you need to help them make a decision to buy.
3. Respect time—theirs and yours. Your standard reply, no matter what their response, "Have a nice day."
4. If you do not know the answer, be honest. Ask for a

phone number and get back to them with the information. You need their phone and fax number for your database, anyway.

5. Take clear messages and get all the information you need to do your homework for the client.

6. Listen for their tone . . . if you have disturbed them, apologize. If they are ill, think how you could help.

While speaking on the telephone you will achieve the highest and greatest impact by exactly matching the tone of the person on the other line. That means, if they are speaking quickly, speak quickly. If they are speaking slowly, speak slowly. If they are yelling, but they like you, yell back. If they are yelling because they don't like you, "Have a nice day," should be your only answer.

Voice modulation and inflections are also important in telephone magic. If a person has a high pitched voice, you must also match your voice. If a low pitched voice, respond with a low pitched voice. The stronger the projection of who you are over the phone, the shorter the interview time will be with them.

Always match and mirror the client for the fastest results. Always ask for the appointment over the phone. Your tone is only one of concern for the client. Learn to give positive reposes for negative questions. Try to solve their problems.

The premise is that it takes five times more time and money to get a new client than it does to keep an old one. Not only is it much more fun to keep in contact with someone you already know and have a pleasant working relationship with, but it is much more profitable. It's like calling up old friends just to say, "Hello".

Every client you have in your data base should be

contacted by phone, at least quarterly, to see what's new. You never know when Aunt Matilda died and they now can afford to buy your product or your service. You never know if the corporation had a merger and now needs your services. You never know if there has been a material change to require your product/service.

The reasons you call past clients are:

1.  To ask for referrals
2.  To educate and inform
3.  To advise about any internal changes you have had
4.  To advise about your latest new product, service or promotion.

Just check in to see how they are. You'll be amazed how much they love to hear from you once you make the effort to call. They will be raving fans of your accomplishments. When you are upset or have had a bad week, there is nothing like a raving fan to adore you and to help you to cheer up.

Start calling again, you'll have more business than you can possibly manage. The more often that you communicate, the more often they believe that you actually care about them.

If you own a small business, office or health office, your staff should be calling all clients, past and present at least one hour every day. The energy this creates relates to volume in your business and creating the perception that you care for your clients.

Telemarketing costs no money. Every office has a phone. Each assistant, associate, or employee has at least twenty minutes of fill-in time a day when they could make twenty calls. If each of ten staff members made 20 calls a day, for twenty working days of each month, that results in 4000 calls a month. How many transactions could that be?

- How much energy would that generate in your business?
- How much profit would that generate in your business?
- How much repeat or referral business would that generate in your business?

Telemarketing is a habit that your company should get into every day, like brushing your teeth or taking a shower. For the health of your business and relationships with your clients keep phoning until someone says, "Yes".

Stay on the phone until you get results. Keep phoning until they say, "YES." Keep phoning until you like it. Keep phoning until you are employed. If you're not phoning, you're not employed.

Whenever sales are slow, accounts are low, or the speed of my business is not where I want it to be—I start dialing for dollars. It ignites my results!

My clients totally love me because they can trust me. They always trust that I will do what I say, because I communicate with them. They love doing business with a friend of their family. That's what I have become, their friend.

### Customers for Life - by Carl Sewell

1. The most important thing we ever did was decide to be the best.
2. If you give your clients a chance to communicate, they will tell you how you can provide them with excellent service.
3. You have to convince your clients that your service is more valuable to them than their money.
4. Under promise and over deliver.
5. People like doing business with you when you keep your word.
6. Always deliver the unexpected extras.
7. Being nice to people is just 20% of doing a great job.

Designing systems that allow you to do the job right the first time every time makes you a star.

8. The key is to develop a system that allows you to give the right results to the client the first time.

9. The best system in the world for providing excellent service is to give the client what you say you are going to do and do it right the first time.

10. Often a customer judges us by the way we handle their problems. What they always remember is what you did for them when something went wrong.

11. Every survey on customer service ever done shows we fix the problem, we have a good chance of maintaining the relationship.

12. Good enough never is. Excellence is what counts.

13. If we want to attract clients and keep the ones we have, we need to give them reasons to do business with us.

14. Set high standards and constantly exceed them.

15. The most important system we could put into practice is one that demands improvement in ourselves.

16. Making improvements up front will often save time in the future.

17. Reward people who frequently do business with you.

18. Measure everything that is important and post the results, so that everyone has a chance to see and compete.

19. Identify your best clients and communicate with them regularly.

20. Analyse what is relevant, post the results and keep raising the level of acceptable performance. Keep raising the standards of excellence.

# THE LAZARUS THEORY
## *Dead Client Walking*

The tools of marketing will give you hundreds, if not thousands, of clients to work with. They are tools that make your business interesting in both range and frequency of results. These secrets of marketing are meant to give you a large volume of clients. The next three chapters will give you secrets for handling some of the personality challenges in your client volume.

Challenging clients are not sent to us to cause us pain or grief, they are sent to cause growth, so that we learn how to handle the situation the next time it comes along—and come along it will. When you begin to have efficient systems not just for office procedure, or client procedure, but for handling difficult client, you find true excellence in your business.

In the Bible, it tells us that as Jesus walked through the towns and villages, creating miracles, many people followed him and believed in his work.

One of these devout followers of Jesus, had just lost his son, Lazerus. Instead of weeping and wailing at the death of his son, he ran to the place where Jesus was speaking and emplored him for his help. Jesus said, "Because of your faith, let this be done for you." Upon the man's return to his village, he did indeed find out that his son had been raised from the dead and was walking towards him.

We can create many miracles in our own businesses, however, we cannot always resurrect the dead client walking, as much as we may wish to do so.

Here are some signs of the dead client, in case you don't sense a pulse.

1.  They rarely, if ever, return your calls. They miss appointments or are late for appointments and never apologize for their behavior. Your constant attention is expected to every detail. It's "me first" with them.

2.  They expect to pay very little, or nothing, for your services whatever that may be. If you charge them less than you would other clients, no matter what you charge, they will run you ragged demanding more services, or say that you did not work hard enough for them in spite of the extra services you gave.

3.  They will get as many bonuses or extras out of your business as they can. Beware that freebies will never make them happy. Misery loves company—they will do what they can to make you as miserable as they are.

4.  In a loud tone of voice, they will publicly discredit you, your company, and it's service after the transaction is complete. After they got more than they should have out of the deal (including your blood or your first born child).

5.  If there are commissions in the transaction they believe that they are entitled to their fair share of them, for keeping you gainfully employed. Commission deduction

is not only a request it is a demand *if* you meet the other impossible guidelines they set in order to keep their loyalty.

6. No matter how professional your ancillary staff is, they will do or say whatever they can to discredit them to the public as well. Rule number 3 applies here as well, after all they are your staff.

7. After you have done all the leg work, all the research, all the hard work to solve their problem, and they know all the answers, they thank you and tell you their brother is also in the business, but thanks for your help anyway.

8. They tell you lie after lie about what they really wanted, then buy something similar to the products you showed them for a higher price than they told you they could afford. Loyalty is not a word in their vocabulary.

If these scenarios sound familiar, then you are in the presence of a dead client walking—all over you. The trick is to know that it is only a game. They want to play you the victim, as long and as hard as possible, without ever giving you what it is that you want out of it, an honest day's pay for an honest day's work.

Recognize that the dead client walking is selfish, insincere, demanding, controlling and totally impossible. He has no more use for you or your services than an extra nose or extra ears, but he will play you to the end because he doesn't respect you. If you allow him to run your business he will, and your life spirit into the ground with it. If you show him courteously what your limits are, he must either adhere to them, or you are best rid of him.

When dealing with this type of client, set your business boundaries early in the transaction. It may mean keeping this client waiting a day or two to return his call, when you finally get a response. It may mean canceling or rescheduling an appointment with this client, once in a while, for someone who actually needs and appreciates your services.

Have faith that the universe will bring you clients who are genuine and sincere in their need for your gifts and talents. Have faith that the dead client walking can only be resurrected when he knows you run the show.

Your answer to this client is to be the good fisherman—catch and release.

There are thousands of great clients who will fuel you both emotionally and financially and thank you for your efforts. Get on with your search for them. When you run an efficient business, where you enjoy your work, your clients, and your business; they will seek you out.

Let the dead client walking be resurrected by someone who is not interested in profitability, but in pain. Martyrdom, is not inclusive requirement in profitability. Get onto the next client, quickly.

# THE TALE OF ST. GEORGE AND THE DRAGON

*Dealing with the Dragon Client*

We are grateful to the knights and other heroes who thoughtlessly rode around killing dragons many years ago, so that we rarely come across a real dragon today. Dragons were astonishingly interesting creatures: part crocodile, part snake, bits of lion, eagle and hawk all thrown in for good measure. Not only did they leap in the air, they flew tremendously far distances and ran at very fast speeds. Dragons were known for being fearless creatures.

Only when they were angry or frightened would they rush about with smoke hissing from their nostrils. When things really got rough, flames came rushing out of their mouths.

The Chinese admired rather than feared the dragon. Dragons guarded the homes of the emperors and the Chinese gods and brought rain to the earth when the crops needed it. That is why paper kites are still flown to this day to honor the dragon.

In the fourth century, when St. George was born,

dragons were still feared rather than admired. They slept in nasty damp caves, often guarding the treasures which they stole from someone else.

They had an unhealthy appetite for eating young princesses, although any young woman made a tasty morsel.

St. George was the most famous dragon slayer of all time. He traveled the kingdoms slaying dragons and spreading the gospel. In the small town of Silne, the people were terrified of the dragon who lived in the cave by a stagnant lagoon on the edge of the town. People came from miles around to see the dragon as they believed him to be responsible for the stench that came into the city. So they began to feed the dragon two sheep a day in the hopes that this pest would go away. Of course the dragon enjoyed this even more . . . now he was getting two meals a day and decided the town's people must really like him to treat him so well. Certainly he had no idea that they were afraid of him.

Eventually the townspeople began to run out of sheep. The council called a meeting to see what the most important people thought they should do. The king himself decided to attend.

"We have given the dragon over one thousand sheep and he still has not gone away," they lamented.

"Perhaps he will never go away," said the minister of internal affairs. "What are we to give it instead?"

The king was very stern and grim as he replied. "It is well known that dragons enjoy the taste of children. We must give him our children instead. Once a week we will feed our children to the dragon to placate him, so that he does not destroy the town."

The result of this decree sent terror into the hearts of the villagers. Then the king spoke again. "Each child in the town will be given a number. Once a week a child will be given to the dragon in order to save the town," he rose to his feet. "That is my law. There will be no exceptions."

Three months passed and a dozen children were sacrificed. Their bones lay outside of the cave as the dragon picked each flavorful morsel. As for the dragon, he had been puzzled at the change in his feeding habits, but enjoyed the tasty morsels. In fact he found the children tasty and delicious and so he stayed longer, yet.

By the time that St. George arrived, an atmosphere of pure poison descended on the mists. Every Tuesday the lottery was held. Parents rushed home after work to see if their child had to be sacrificed next. Then at noon a bell would ring. Soldiers would knock on the house and take the child to the cave. Everywhere else parents were grateful their children were not sacrificed.

St. George came into the palace in the middle of a tempestuous conversation between the king and the minister of external affairs. "You can't," the king said. "I forbid it."

"These were your instructions," said the external affairs minister. "You made the law," said the second. "You said there were no exceptions," said the third.

"But she is a princess and she is my only daughter." Tears were streaming down the face of the king. "When I find the idiot who did this . . .."

"She took her own number, Your Majesty," said the minister of external affairs

Saint George realized there was no time to waste. He left the palace without introducing himself to the king. The lagoon wasn't hard to find, he rode in the direction of the stench. He followed his nose and soon found the dragon.

When he heard weeping he knew that he had arrived at

the right place. He walked into the cave to find the dragon still sleeping, it must have been a long weekend.

When the princess saw the dragon, she thought it was all over.

St. George was not afraid. "Bad dragon," he said. "Do you really mean to eat this little girl?"

As the dragon growled uncertainly, the little princess opened one eye.

"Don't you know that it's wrong to eat people?" he asked the dragon. "Enough of this foolishness!" St. George untied the little girl and led her out of the cave. He took the ribbon from the princess' hair and tied it around the dragon.

"I think you will make a wiser ruler than your father," said St. George. "Your courage has shown us that."

When the dragon returned to the village, the entire town converted to Christianity, as did the dragon. The princess married a handsome prince and they lived happily ever after in a neighboring village.

This is a very cute story and very relevant to situations that actually exist today. The difference between the dragon client and the dead client walking is that the dragon client  will conduct himself to cause you fear. His motives are not good business, his motives are to destroy you, get back at the world, make money out of a law suit, whatever it takes to cause you grief or pain. He feels he is misunderstood or victimized and is bitter at the world.

## SYMPTOMS OF HAVING A DRAGON CLIENT

1. Beware of the smoke screen and much noise. This is a cover-up for being frightened and in pain—all of which he will transfer to you if you let him.
2. Unsettling in his habits, a complete control freak that will change the rules on you no matter how much you

do for him. Will eat you alive if you allow it.

3. Feeds on unsuspecting salespeople and abuses them with invented stories about their imaginary wrong doings.

4. It's important to recognize the dragon client quickly. The stench from the lagoon will get you there. Smell the hidden agenda, first.

5. If you ever do anything to anger the dragon client more than he has already been angered by someone else, beware your professional designation. He'll expect it to be his right to have that too.

6. The anger does not go away quickly. In short he will tell the world about you.

7. The only way to protect yourself from the dragon client is to arm yourself with as much technology, facts, history and research as you possibly can. Set your boundaries and limits. Get your facts straight.

8. Approach the dragon client from the intellectual side. Let the smoke diffuse. When the anger has been vented, present your case from a logical point of view.

9. If you cannot intellectualize the dragon client into submission, sacrifice your petty agenda to win and let him fume at someone else. You and your reputation will be mincemeat if you don't.

10. When all else fails, call your lawyer and stop this wing nut in his tracks. His only agenda is to get money from you in whatever disreputable way he can.

11. Remember, this energy is not making you any money. This is what the dragon client wants. Remember you "nasty salesperson" are not to profit from your work; he is. All of this effort is negative energy, go out and get three clients that love you for all you do and leave the crusade of changing the dragon client's behaviour to some other unsuspecting soul that enjoys the pain.

Dragon clients come in some amazing disguises. As a realtor I experienced several dragons. The key is to recognize them by nature earlier in the transaction and protect yourself legally first.

* I had a client who had the written credentials of 'millionaire status' default on a rent payment after he trashed the house. I paid all costs with my reputation as the other client had a long standing relationship with my boss. My client made him look foolish, also.

* One client was a business consultant who broke every agreement we made in order to make me look like a liar and discredit my reputation. Not only did I forfeit my paycheck, I looked like a total fool to my colleagues who said, "Where is your contract? Why would you begin without a contract? Get it in writing first or walk away."

* A lawyer charged eight thousand dollars to close a transaction leaving no money for the commissions. Highway robbery? Because he dispersed the funds, other than a law suit, there was no recourse.

* Another client went to the media for an incorrect advertisement of her property because I only had her verbal permission. She also had told my broker, she had given me permission. I had done everything possible to help this client . . . her only motive was money. She called every professional designation. She called head office. She called the newspapers. She called the media. It was a no-win situation causing embarrassment to me, my colleagues, my office—public humiliation at worst. Not only was there wasted time, there was wasted money in legal actions on our part afterwards.

Do not compromise your principles or your standards

for the dragon client. This client is sent to teach you many lessons on stretching your abilities as a salesperson or a company.

Turn this dragon client around quickly with facts, logic, or technology or turn yourself around and get out fast.

The earlier in the transaction that you protect your professional status, the better. If you cannot do so before this reaches full fledged escalated war seek legal council.

Whatever you fight to get, you fight to keep. When you are not in harmony with yourself and your standards, you cannot attract the type of clients you need to do really great business.

Taking a stand is not only necessary to your self esteem, it is necessary to your survival and the future of your business.

Letting anyone grind you down, does nothing to polish your business performance. It does make you wiser, stronger and more cautious in dealing with the public that has a hidden agenda.

Learn to get all agreements in writing. Never regret these clients in your past. Embrace them as the teachers they are.

# LOYALTY FOR LIFE

*You Don't Want the Business*
*~ The Tale of the Ugly Wife*

The tale is set at the time of King Arthur, the legendary king that ruled over the knights of the round table. King Arthur's famous nephew, Sir Gawain is the noblest of Arthur's knights and accompanies him on the quest. The tale begins as is customary (of the time) with the rescue of a damsel in distress. Her husband has been enslaved by the wicked knight of Tarn Wathelyne.

The sight of this poor woman so moved King Arthur that he set out that very day to find the knight at this castle and to see what he could do to get her husband back for her (now there's customer service for you). As King Arthur had never known fear, he went alone, armed with his spear and trusty sword Excalibur.

As he rode, deeper and deeper into the woods, he passed a lake as dark as blood in the night. His body shivered. When he saw the knights castle, and heard the knight crunching his footsteps on the gravel, fear struck him.

Minutes seemed like hours as the knight approached him. The voice that followed was as cold as death itself.

"So you are the great King Arthur," it whispered. "Tell me why I should spare your life?"

"You are the devil!" King Arthur gasped feverishly. King Arthur trembled with anger at how easily he had deceived.

"Have pity on me," he begged.

"Because it would be too easy to kill you now in your vulnerable state, I will spare your life on one condition, that you return to this same place a year from today with the answer to the following question. If you answer correctly your life will be saved. If you answer incorrectly, your bones will decorate the walls of my castle.

You will die a slow painful death."

The knight laughed insidiously, "I want to know, what is it that women want most in the world?" With that, he disappeared with a fling of his cape. Horses hooves were heard in the distance. The noble knight Gawain had by this time ridden up to the scene. He was concerned when he saw the king leaving the kingdom with his sword alone.

"Black magic caused you fear," Gawian cried. "By your leave, Sire, I will ride with you to the castle and we can make short order of this jokester."

"I am honour bound to pursue this quest," King Arthur sighed. "What is it that women want most in the world? I have a year to find out."

"Then I will come with you," promised Gawain. Together they rode out into the country far and wide. They found more answers that they knew what to do with. Most of the women desired good husbands, loving children and some luxuries.

Luxury, immortality, independence, these were all answers that rang true, but these were not good enough to answer the question.

Time passed quickly, days passed into months, months

into seasons and seasons into a year. They knew that they had still not found the real answer.

Although they had catalogues of answers in their saddlebags, they knew in their hearts that they had failed.

On the day before, they were to go back to face the Black Knight, they met an old woman in the clearing. She sat beside a stream peacefully reading a book. As Gawain approached her, he noticed that she was beautifully dressed.

As she turned her head, he gasped as he realized that she was the ugliest woman he had ever seen. She was so ugly, that he shuddered to lay his eyes on her. She was hideously fat, horrible skin with warts, teeth rotten and sticking out, with a bad suint in her eye. But, as she was a woman, and the only woman that they could see, Gawain approached her courteously.

He approached her with a deep respectful bow. King Arthur also decided to ask her the question that had no answer, but before he could speak, she addressed him in a screech.

"I know the question that you are going to ask me," she screeched, "and I also know the answer. But I will give it to you on one condition only."

"And what would that be?" King Arthur demanded to know.

The horrible looking woman licked her lips and smacked them in the direction of the handsome Gawain.

"That knight . . ." she said, giggling. "I rather fancy having him for my husband. If you give him to me, I will tell you the answer that you seek. I will save your life and your kingdom, King Arthur."

Hearing these words, Gawain went pale. He was indeed young and handsome. What would his friends say if they saw

him come home with this monster?

Even as he contemplated his own demise, he realized that he had a duty to his uncle, his king and his kingdom.

"My Lord, if this woman can save your life . . ."

"I can, I can . . ." crooned the ugly crone.

" . . . then I will gladly marry her."

"I couldn't let you do that my dear nephew."

"You cannot stop me," Gawain retorted. With that he fell on one knee and asked the crone for her hand in marriage, if she would tell the king what it was that women (clients, customers) desire most in the world.

"What do you desire, woman, you shall have."

The very next morning the king rode back to the castle of Tarn Wathelyne.

Again, the same sense of evil overcame him, but this time he was prepared for it and rode forth in confidence. The Black Knight was waiting as King Arthur rode up to him with his sword unsheathed.

"Well, king?" he growled. "Tell me the answer to the question. What do women (clients, customers) want most in the world?"

King Arthur replied clearly and boldly in return. "It is this," he said, "That they should have their will and they should rule over men."

For a second the Black knight was silent. Then he dropped to his knees in apology. "You have answered correctly," he said, "by doing so you have broken the spell that the evil witch, Morgana le Fay cast over me. As her black magic ended, sire, I may now serve you at the Round Table. Beneath this horrible armour, I am a good man and will prove myself worthy."

With those words the castle at Tarn Wathelyne crumbled and the ground swallowed it up. As sunlight broke through the clouds, the birds began to sign.

The two knights and the king rode back to the kingdom to prepare for the wedding.

## THE WEDDING

The marriage of the handsome Sir Gawain to the ugly old woman was an event that no one would forget. The woman giggled all through the service. At the end of the vows, she belched loudly so that everyone could hear as she accepted the knights hand in marriage.

During the feast afterward, the woman spilled more food down the front of her dress than most guests ate. She got drunk on the wine, told rude and obnoxious jokes to the guests. She stumbled everywhere. The guests congratulated Gawain on the luck of his fortune with as much sincerity as they could muster.

They laughed as little as possible.

Poor Gawain was the politest of all. He called her "My Lady" at every turn.

He was quieter than usual and continued to behave as though nothing was wrong.

At the end of the evening, when he was finally alone with his bride, watching her powder her nose, or the warts on her chin, it was finally too much for him.

When he burst into tears, the old crone asked, "What is it, my little plum?"

"Lady," Gawain relied. "I can no longer conceal my thoughts from you. I do not want to offend you, but you are very ugly, old and evidently of low birth. Forgive me, I can only speak the truth."

"What is wrong with being honest?" the lady gushed. "With age comes wisdom and discretion. Are these not good qualities for a wife to possess? Maybe I am ugly, but you will never fear any rivals. Finally, you accuse me of being of low birth. Are you really such a snob, Gawain? Do you think that nobility comes of birth born into a good family? Surely, it is the character of the person that matters, not just the size of their castle, the number of the Arabians in the barn and the number of sheep in the field? Can you not teach me to be noble like you?"

With those words, Gawain paused in thought. He felt very ashamed at treating her so terribly. After all, this woman had saved his uncle and the kingdom. He had behaved badly not fitting for a knight of the Round Table.

"My Lady," he said, "you are right in everything that you have said. I sincerely apologize for speaking to you so discourteously."

"Then join me now," she whispered softly to him. Even as she spoke, Gawain detected something different in her voice. As he turned around to glance at her in the candlelight, he was astonished to see how she had changed. A beautiful young woman lay in his bed, her eyes glowing with the eagerness of a bride, her skin shining on her wedding night.

"Let me explain," she said. "I was also under the enchantment of the evil queen, Morgana Le Fay. I could help my brother release your uncle from the terrible spell that had been cast over him, but only a kind and understanding noble spirit, could save me from this horrible enchantment. I am your wife, if you will have me. This time the choice is your own."

With that Gawain took her hand in his and proposed. They were married the next day to the amazement of all the court.

How does this story refer to the client?

1. What the client desires most in the world is to have their own will. Under your guidance the client should always get their own way. Listen to the client.

2. The client needs to feel in control of his needs and wants. It is the responsibility of the salesperson or the company that his wishes are fulfilled.

3. Opportunities sometimes present themselves in blue jeans or as ugly old crones.

4. It is not always the presentation of the opportunity that is important, but rather the timing of the transaction in all cases. There was only one day left to solve the problem. There are always solutions to problems when the timing is right.

5. Sometimes it is only our attitude to the situation that needs to be changed, rather than the situation itself. Gawain needed a wife. This woman solved his major problems. Her appearance or her lack of breeding or wealth were irrelevant.

6. When Gawain listened to the tone of the ugly wife and noticed that it had changed, he had to change his outlook. Sometimes tone is more indicative of the transaction, than the actual transaction. Listen to tone.

7. The loyalty of the representative of the company, the knight was to the king (as the CEO) from the beginning. When the innermost needs of the client were respected, the kingdom gained stature.

8. As the client is revered in the transaction and cared for, the loyalty to the representative of the company was won. The ugly old crone was transformed to a creature of beauty. The woman became his client for life.

9. The difference between the dead client walking, the dragon client and the ugly old crone is that the ugly old

crone actually intended to do whatever it took to complete the transaction. The ugly old crone had loyalty to the representative of the company. The ugly old crone would give referrals forever.

10. At the end of the day, when the shining noble knight extended his manners beyond his own boundaries and began to listen to the crone's words, he understood her purpose. Only then did he have a client for life. As he turned his back on the client and listened to tone, he gave the negotiation room to breathe, and thus won the heart of the client.

You break the separations that divide the parties, in order to create loyalty, you do not break the parties—or force them to marry you.

# THE FOOL WHO IS
# SILENT PASSES FOR WISE

## *The Tale of Narcissus*

This secret is for all salesmen or women, who in their exuberance to sell the product, neglect to learn the secret of silence. The tale of Narcissus, is the story of the most beautiful young man in all of Ancient Greece, at least in the opinion of Narcissus.

Every morning as he awoke, he would examine himself in the full length mirror, running his hand through his long blonde curls. He would wink at himself daily in the mirror.

His parents, had no idea, what to do with him. At sixteen, he was remarkably beautiful. Half the girls in the country had fallen in love with him. As he spoke to them his voice being so sultry he could seduce the most unwilling maiden.

One girl swore that she would kill herself if Narcissus would not be kinder to her. His response was to send her the sword.

But, it was not only mortals that fell in love with Narcissus. It was also the spirits, and the nymphs that haunted the glades and the rivers and guarded the trees in the forests. Trees were often considered gods in the days of the Greeks.

One of these spirits was Echo. Falling in love with Narcissus was the worst mistake in her life. When she met Narcissus, she was unable to tell him how she felt about him, she could only use his words. The result was disastrous.

One day when she met him in the forest, he had been out hunting stags. As he wandered down a path he was lost on, he noticed the nymph gazing nervously at him. He yawned.

"Hello," he muttered. "I suppose you're yet another of these women that find me so very attractive."

"So very attractive," Echo replied.

"I thought so," Narcissus said. "Well, your wasting your time, I'm afraid."

"I'm afraid," Echo said.

"And so you ought to be," Narcissus continued. "To be absolutely honest, if you were Aphrodite herself, I wouldn't come near you."

"Come near me!" Echo cried.

"Are you deaf or something? I just told you I wouldn't. Now go away!"

"Go away!" Echo moaned.

Realizing that her plight was hopeless, the nymph fled from the woods, tears streaming down her cheeks. She spent the rest of her life heartbroken and alone in a desolate valley, living in a cave. Soon all that was left of her was her voice. Should you ever find yourself alone in a valley and call out, Echo will always answer you, in her heart she is still mourning for Narcissus.

It would never happen in the 90's. Someone would have given her a copy of Barbara De Angelis's brilliant book *Are You the One for Me?* and she would have realized that one-sided relationships don't work.

Meanwhile, Narcissus continued on his merry way. Unfortunately, the gods have a way of getting even. Aphrodite, the goddess of love, heard his cruel remarks to Echo. By his words and his deeds, Narcissus had made himself love's enemy. Aphrodite, therefore, put a curse on him making him fall in love with himself.

On his way home, passing by a crystal clear pool of water, he knelt down to take a drink. What he saw was the most beautiful boy in the world smiling back at him. He smiled. The boy smiled. He had fallen in love with his own reflection.

The next day his parents who had been searching for him found him beside the pool of water.

"Narcissus," they cried. "What are you doing? We've been so worried about you."

"Hush," replied Narcissus. "You'll frighten him away."

"Frighten away who?" asked his mother.

"That boy," Narcissus replied. "He is so beautiful and yet so cruel. For when I reach out to try to kiss him, he runs away from me. But he comes back after a while. See there he is now," Narcissus continued with a dreamy look in his eyes.

"Come into the house, now," replied his mother, "You'll catch your death of cold, sitting out here in the night air."

"No! No!" Narcissus cried. "I can't leave him. Not ever!"

Despite everything that his parents said, Narcissus refused to move. All day and all night he lay in the long grass admiring his own reflection. His parents brought him food. He wouldn't touch it. His torment became worse because the object of his love was only inches away from him at all times, yet, they could never meet, they could never touch.

Narcissus fell in love with a reflection in the pool, not

because it talked his head off, but rather because it was silent and an mirror image of himself.

At last the pain became too much for him. It seemed that the boy in the pool had also suffered excruciatingly, for his eyes also seemed red and sore.

In the only act of true and unselfish love that Narcissus was ever to commit, he reached into his belt for the dagger that he carried there.

"I have hurt you as much as you have hurt me," Narcissus whispered. With that he drew his dagger and said, "I shall hurt you no more."

As he plunged the dagger into his heart, he screamed; the boy screamed too.

Somewhere in the distance, Echo cried out, too.

Narcissus died. Aphrodite, taking pity on him turned his body into a flower as a reminder of what had happened.

To this day, narcissus flowers can be found growing wild beside silent pools.

This story is not a literal translation in unselfish customer service, or having a product "that is to die for." It is a story about a salesman that thought so much of himself, that he forgot about the needs of others (i.e. the client).

Salespeople are known for blithering on at the mouth about their latest deal, or the latest product, the difficulties or victories of the latest transaction, the multimillions of dollars of production, their latest unbelievable new purchase with all the money they made on an impossible deal. On and on and on.

The client in the meantime is left on the sidelines in stunned silence wondering when he will be noticed.

I have been fortunate to work in high powered offices with brilliant salespeople. These people are so talented that they can produce as much income in one week or one month as many people earn in one year. I know, because I've done it myself.

Salespeople come to believe that they are immortal, a gift to the gods in their abilities and their skills. However, just like Narcissus, they must understand the wrath of the gods, or the market, or their competitors will cause their demise. Unless you are a paid professional speaker, this behavior is uncalled for and detrimental to business. If you are in a management capacity, the same rules ring true, in your conversation with staff—less is more.

Narcissus fell in love at the silent pool because of it's silence and because the pool was a reflection of himself. That is the secret of winning the heart of the customer is to remain silent in deference to their needs. Becoming a reflection of the customer's wishes will win you the heart of your client. As a result, you win in any market and your business will always be booming. You never have to worry about where the next client will come from. When you win a client's heart, the transaction lasts forever. The by-product is they tell all their friends about you—resulting in residual income.

What goes up, frequently comes down. Just as Aphrodite did not forget the words of Narcissus when he was in his power, Narcissus would never forget the situation of his own ego that caused his demise.

Sometimes it is better to be silent and modest in success, than boastful and bragging. The "silent fool interested only in the needs of the other person always passes for wise." The silent fool reflecting the mirror image of the client wins the heart of the client and their loyalty for life.

# PRACTICE, PRACTICE, PRACTICE

How does one get good at practicing the tools of "Secrets"? The same way you get good at practicing the piano, learning to play tennis, skiing, or doing anything else you love. Practice, practice, practice.

Once you're truly convinced that the secrets in this book can help your business begin to apply them. Read this book as often as you need to understand how easy business really can be, then practice the principles as much as possible.

Don't expect to get everything right the first time. Life is lived by trial and error. The secrets that work for you may not work for your neighbour, your brother or your competitor.

If the "Secrets" don't work for you the first time, don't despair, maintain your practice sessions. Eventually you'll get the knack of making your business a raging success and your clients raving fans for your service.

Practice convincing everyone to see life your way. Practice convincing everyone to help you get what you really want—financial freedom. Help enough people to get what they want and you will get what you want.

Reread "Secrets" as often as possible to remember that all business is relationship. Keep the old relationships so that you may get referrals and repeat clients.

Use the phone to keep in touch as often as you can. A thirty second voice mail is better than no communication at all. Pursue, pursue, pursue all the elements of promotion, marketing and business plans to get the results you need in your business or corporation.

When we change our definition of gratifying relationships to be long lasting and mutual, not short term and hurtful our energy in our business goes up progressively.

When we absorb and use "Secrets" we set boundaries with clients so they recognize us as the professionals we really are. Getting overly friendly, putting off asking for the order or the contract is detrimental to our good business health.

Our clients are actually more impressed when we have a life outside of our business, and keep our commitments to our families first. Well-rounded people keep their lives healthy and balanced.

If you think that the "Secrets" are a manual for life rather than simply secrets for good business, you might read and act on them more often. Then you will have plenty of clients to practice with forever.

# PROFITABILITY TO DIE FOR

## *The Tale of Achilles*

The Achilles Heel in any story has always been the strongest link in the chain. We believe it to be the weakest, but as any myth, the theory is completely false. We learn from it, if we pay attention to the riddle of Achilles.

Achilles was the son of the God of Thetis and Peleus. This god was an immortal. As an immortal she was furious that she was forced to be married to a mortal man because children would also be mortal. She cried about her fate. She was very upset that she would live to see both her children and her husband grow old and she would outlive them all as an immortal and never age.

In her revenge at this curse, Thetis took the baby, Achilles, just after he was born and dipped him into the River of Immortality, the Styx. All of the baby's body parts were completely immersed in this river, except for the back of his heel, where his mother held onto him. In that one moment, the child Achilles, became immortal. All except his heel, the only mortal part of his body where his mother hung onto him.

Achilles grew up to be a very formidable warrior. He demanded respect and honor. One day someone who had secretly watched Thetis dip her son into the Styx told the enemy Paris to manufacture a poison arrow to kill Achilles. Once shot in the only part of his body that was mortal, Achilles died almost immediately, a quick and painless death.

Likewise in any business, the Achilles heel, the weakest link in the chain occurs. We believe in our own immortality, that is, current "great" market conditions will cause us to be invulnerable to the ravages of the last economic battle. Not so. Like Achilles, no matter how great a warrior we have become in winning in the ravages of the markets and earning our own current market share, unless we are protected, in the area of profitability, we too shall die.

Profitability, therefore is the Achilles Heel of any business. No matter how great or how small the income is, our profitability margins, and our expenses will make us or break us in the final analysis. I have watched several entrepreneurs lose their fortunes several times over in their disrespect for the bottom line and profitability margins. There are stock markets that overestimate reserves, resources, capital, or labor costs and the stocks plummet and die. Millionaires with huge budgets, overestimating good fortune in a current market repeatedly approach bankruptcy without close examination of the bottom line—profitability. It never matters how much you earn, whether it is thousands, hundreds of thousands or millions. It only matters how much you keep. Net, net, net. After the tax department, after the expenses, after the employees are paid, how much are you really bringing home? Are you earning less than the employees, or more? Is that how it's supposed to be?

Remembering the Achilles heel will make you the strongest chain in the link because you will always know where your weaknesses are most evident.

Learning to search for what could be poisoning your business, or looking for enemies that you have either within the ranks as energy leakages or as unnecessary expenses will clarify the money streams. Unless you have justification and solid evidence of a return for your investment into the business, learn not to spend, waste, or misuse funds that could otherwise make your business profitable. That expenditure will become your downfall. Rather than winning the war on profitability the Achilles heel of unnecessary expense will be your demise. Both you and your business will die an quick and painful death.

Examine expenses, whatever or whoever consistently costs you income with no return must be removed. You should be looking for a 4:1 profitability ratio on all expenses. Amounts greater than this can be achieved if you carefully examine every expense for return on investment. There is no second guessing about the consequences of a slow leak. Just as Achilles, lost his life force energy with the poisoned arrow striking his bloodstream, so your business will lose it's life force energy with any expense that does not promote a 4:1 return. Profitability levels increase dramatically with increased use of the telephone or broadcast letters to prospect certain market niches.

The day you learn to be brutally consistent with this one secret is the day that your profitability will soar from less than 10% to an average of 50% or higher. It doesn't matter when you begin to look at your profitability, or even where you cut expenses, only that you consistently look at profitability with every expense. Cut everything that is not essential for growth. Like pruning a tree, the more you cut one season, the hardier and more consistent the growth will be the next season. Cut and replace in the areas that are currently profitable. Keep investing where and with whom you consistently see patterns of return. Cease and remove consistent losses immediately.

The Achilles Heel of profitability will either cause your business to prosper, or to die. Examination and introspection will help you to look for Achilles heel in your business. No one can make those decisions for you, only you know what really needs to stay and who or what must be pruned for maximum growth.

When you've made the decision stick with it—growth will follow. Take the earned funds that you've now found and put them back into product, people or services that will enhance you. In this way your profitability will continue to sky-rocket, and your Achilles heel will indeed become a myth.

# IS YOUR BUSINESS RUNNING YOU?

## *The Midas Touch*

Midas, the king of Phrygia was rich. Everyone said that he was born to be rich. As a child, ants carried grains of wheat to his mouth so that he would never be hungry. The palace seers believed that the little prince was destined to be one of the richest kings in the world.

It's unfortunate that today we don't believe that we have the right to riches and abundance. Wealth shows up in our lives only with a great deal of pain, turmoil, or heartache. Whatever you truly believe will show up exactly as you expect it to whether you believe good or bad, you are always right. The universe gives us our expectations and beliefs. There are many stories of wealth around us (from rags to riches) if we choose to be inspired and believe we can also accomplish greatness.

Midas believed he was entitled to great wealth and so it appeared for him in the opportunities that were presented to him. One day as Midas was walking in the garden, he found a fat old man lying in the grass under the rose bushes.

This reveler had strayed into the palace grounds the night before to sleep off the effects of too much wine.

Rather than have him thrown off the premises for trespassing, King Midas invited him to stay at the palace to tell him wonderful stories that amused the king. It turned out that this stranger was none other than Silenus, the companion and mentor of Dionysus, the great god.

When Dionysus heard that Midas had been taking care of his old friend and had treated him with respect and care, he was so impressed that he granted Midas any wish that he could fulfill.

One of the secrets of truly great people is that they treat everyone with care. It does not matter who they are or who they appear to be. The Midas touch of wealth begins with concern for anyone who needs help.

Remember that Midas already was the richest man in all the world at that point.

One needs to ask the question "How much better can this get?"

Midas in all his wisdom had no ambition but to become even richer. Without a second thought he replied to the messenger:

"Give thanks to your master, the great Dionysus, and tell him that my dearest wish would be to have everything that I touch turn into pure gold."

When Dionysus heard this request, he frowned.

"Foolish wish," he responded, "and he will be sorry for it." Then, shrugging his shoulders he added, "But if that's what he wants, let him have it. Men should learn to wish for the right things."

The next day Midas was walking in the palace grounds again. Idly he broke off a twig from a low growing tree. It immediately turned into pure gold and glittered with radiance.

"My wish has been granted," he exclaimed. "How wonderful and what wealth I will finally have! Why, I shall be the richest man in the world!"

Scarcely able to believe his good fortune, Midas reached down to pick up a stone, with that the stone became gold. All became gold at his touch. Midas's delight knew no bounds. As soon as he got back to the palace, he ordered that a great feast be prepared to thank Dionysus for his good fortune.

That's the next secret of the wealthy, they are always grateful to whomever helps them. They verbally and openly express their gratitude.

The banquet was prepared. Midas sat at the head of the table surrounded by his adoring courtiers.

"Let us eat and drink," he cried, "and give thanks to the great god, Dionysus."

Looking around at his assembled company, his face lit up in smiles. As he took a piece of bread and raised it to his lips, it turned to solid gold. The smile died on his face. He put out his hand to touch meat. It too became gold. In his desperation, he reached out for a goblet of wine to quench his thirst. As soon as the wine touched his lips, a stream of gold began to flow down his throat. At last he realized that everything he tried to eat or to drink would also turn to gold.

He also realized that he must soon face death by starvation. How much would he give just to taste a stale crust of bread or a cup of water.

The courtiers were upset. "The king is ill," they sighed, "let us leave him to himself and go home."

So the guests departed, leaving Midas pale and distracted.

"Oh, what a fool I have been," sighed Midas. "This

golden touch will be the ruin of me, yet. What is the use of all the gold in the world, if I am to die from lack of food and water?"

Midas raised his arms to the sky and begged the gods to be merciful for his foolish request and take away the power that he had been granted.

Dionysus could see that Midas had learned his lesson and he forgave him. "Go unhappy king, to the country of Lydia. There you will find the River Pactolus. When you have found it, wash your head and your body in it's streams in order that you be cleansed, both of your desire for unlimited wealth and for your punishment."

Midas rushed to do the bidding of the god. When he had washed himself thoroughly, to his infinite relief, he found he had lost the golden touch.

Midas felt that he had just awoken from a bad dream; not only had he lost all his desire for riches, but the precious metal became an object of loathing to him, rather than delight.

***Let's look at the secrets in this myth:***

1. Too much of a good thing is not necessarily better.
2. Both pride and greed cause us to fall in the estimation of our community and our God.
3. Midas abandoned everything for the pursuit of more wealth. It was detrimental to his health, his welfare, his court, his very existence.
4. Enough is sometimes just that.
5. What we want in our human desires is not always in our best interests. It is wiser to wait for the will of the universe, or of our God, before we choose to want more of the same.
6. Material wealth is not all that it's cracked up to be. All

that glitters is not just gold.

7. Midas's business was running him, because he abandoned all else for the pursuit of gold. Under everything is still the need for our health and our humanity. Sometimes the risks in business extend beyond the financial into the loss of health, of family, of respect, or finally the loss of life.

Is it worth it? Is your business running you?

# BE PROUD OF WHO YOU ARE

## *The Millar, His Son and The Ass*

A miller and his son were taking their donkey to the fair to sell him.

"Look at that," cried a cluster of girls they met on the road, "did you ever see such nonsense? What fools they are to be walking along beside the ass instead of riding on him!"

The old man hearing this, quietly asked his son to get on the donkey and walked along with him. Presently a group of very old men came along who walked to together.

"There," said one of them, "that proves exactly what I was saying. The youth of today have no respect for old age. Do you see that idle young man riding while his old father walks?"

"Get down you good for nothing," said another, 'so that your poor old father may rest himself on his weary way."

Upon these comments the father made his son dismount and got up on the donkey, but they had not travelled far when they came upon a gaggle of women and children.

"Why, you lazy old man!" cried several women. "How can you ride on this donkey while this poor lad can hardly keep up beside you? Don't you know that this is child abuse?"

The good natured miller took up his son behind him and they rode in this manner until they reached the town.

"Pray, my dear friend," said a townsman, "is that ass your own?" He was the head of an animal rights activist movement.

"Yes," replied the old man.

"By the way that you loaded him up,one would not have thought so," said the another. "Why you two fellows are more able to carry the poor animal than he is able to carry you!"

So jumping down with his son, they tied the ass's legs to a heavy branch which they carried on their shoulders and so got ready to carry the donkey over a bridge that led to the town. They were now respecting the rights of the animal by carrying him.

This was such an entertaining sight to the townspeople that crowds ran out to see this situation. At that very moment, the ass not liking the noise, broke the cords that bound him and tumbled off the branch into the river below and drowned.

Annoyed and upset, the old man made his way home, convinced that by endeavouring to please everyone, he had pleased no one and lost his ass in the bargain.

This quaint story from Aesop illustrates again, how important your travelling companions are on the road to excellence. If you take anyone's advise along the road and compromise your dignity like the miller, you please no one, least of all yourself, and "lose your ass" in the bargain.

Beware of taking advice from passersby along the road.

Beware of pleasing everyone and not gaining from the result in the end. Shed the shackles of self and focus on your higher purpose.

Being outstanding is not just skill, it takes heart. In the willingness to contribute, to make a difference to society, to commit to excellence, there is the magical path to success. It is found within each of us and within our travelling companions when there is integrity and high standards of performance. The wonderful path of excellence takes us beyond the township of the ordinary into the never-never land of contributing to society.

Contributing to excellence every day transforms every interaction along that path and captures the magic of our existence with our contemporaries.

# NEGOTIATION THE THOR SLEDGE HAMMER MYTH

## *or The Count of Monte Cristo Chisel*

hor was a Viking God, the God of thunder. He was tall with a flowing red beard. Thor was known as the strongest of the Viking Gods. It was said by the Vikings that the sound of thunder was nothing more than the wheels of Thor's chariot rumbling over the clouds.

Thor possessed a pair of iron gloves and a magic belt that doubled his strength. His voice was so loud that it could be heard over the clamor of battle and had his enemies quaking in their boots with terror.

Thor's most prized possession was his hammer Mjolinar . . . called the Destroyer. Thor used his hammer to break the ice of the winter to allow spring to come again. Indeed, his hammer was used to win the most formidable battles in any war.

Thor won most battles of negotiation through intimidation, fierce anger and a booming voice. When that did not help him get his own way, Thor threw his mighty hammer to finalize the negotiations. Brut force and brut strength were the order of the day in finalizing any negotiations that Thor acquired.

Although this is a technique that may work if you are in the construction business, mining industry, or other profession where brut strength is admired, it is not necessarily the case for corporate negotiation.

The tools of excellent negotiation do not come from the use of iron gloves, a magic belt, a booming voice or a hammer slammed down when all else fails. Neither the average consumer, or the corporate executive appreciates this slam dunk style of negotiation where there is only one option—Do it my way!

The tools required for brilliant negotiation are more in line with the techniques of the Count of Monte Cristo. This count was wrongfully accused and spent many years in prison. Rather than shouting about the injustices that had been caused against him, he spent years chiseling away quietly inside the prison walls and eventually escaped a free man.

The tools required for excellent negotiation are more fine tuned. They require a command of all the facts. They require a list of technical details. They require a past history of negotiation that preceded the transaction. They require the trust of both parties.

When these tools are employed the strategy to excellent negotiation must be set and staged to reach agreement. It is in the best interest of the negotiation of both parties to:

1.  Decide to bring the parties together in a manner that is Win/Win.
2.  Set all thoughts of financial compensation aside . . . What's in it for the clients?

3. Be fair in the decision making processes that lead to the negotiation.

4. Have all the facts, figures and documentation at hand before the negotiation proceeds.

5. Work in the interests of the parties not in the interests of the salesperson.

7. Maintain a cool disposition not the anger or manipulation of Thor.

8. Where agreement cannot be reached immediately give the deal room to breathe.

9. Listen to the tone of the parties before ending the negotiations.

10. Never let the negotiations end on your side. Be responsible for bringing the parties together a little at a time.

11. Use the chisel of the Count of Monte Cristo in fine-tuning the negotiations.

12. The see-saw of successful negotiations happens in both sides understanding the motives of the other party.

13. Play the player. If one party is Thor counter the negotiation like Thor.

14. If the other party is like the Count of Monte Cristo act like the Count in the delicacy of the transaction.

15. A sense of humor wins the day.

16. Never count your money when you're sitting at the table, there's time enough for counting when the dealings done.

# LAST BUT NOT LEAST

## *Pandora's Box Secret*

*L*ong, long ago the Greek God Zeus asked Hephaestus, a blacksmith to forge him a woman. Hephaestus, not wanting to offend the god of the gods, molded her out of clay with his own hands. He commissioned all the four winds to breathe life into her and asked the goddesses to dress her in the finest clothing and jewels. This woman was called Pandora.

Pandora was asked to marry a certain, King Epimetheus, the only Titan that did not join in the war against Zeus. Although Epimetheus did not trust the gifts of Zeus, Pandora was a very beautiful woman who captivated any room full of people where she was present. Whatever she did was greeted with great applause. Epimetheus was proud to be married to her.

Epimetheus owned a very large ebony box which was kept in a special room in the palace. In this box he had imprisoned, as a precaution, anything or any emotion that could harm mankind. It was the one room in the palace, that Pandora was absolutely forbidden to enter. Of course it was the one room, that Pandora wanted to enter most because of her overwhelming curiosity.

"Why don't you let me look inside?" she asked.

"It's not for you, my dear," Epimetheus would reply, "You should not look at it."

"But . . ."

"No, no, my dear. No one may open that box."

"Then you don't love me," Pandora pouted. "I'm not going to love you anymore."

They had this conversation many times, until the day that Pandora couldn't resist her curiosity anymore. Despite everything that Epimetheus had told her, she still believed that the box was full of treasures beyond compare.

Waiting until her husband was out of town on a crusade, she stole the key from beside his bed. After all, she was the king's wife and mistress of the house.

Trembling, she knelt beside the box. It was so much smaller than she thought, very old and musty smelling.

Pandora was sure that the box contained untold treasures that the king was too miserly to give her. She was sure that it contained diamonds, pearls and many jewels. She turned the key and out flew all the evil in the world.

One moment she was standing in front of the box, and the next moment out flew hard work, old age, unemployment, taxes, sarcasm, cynicism, violence, war, persecution, insomnia, obesity, fast food, drug addictions, insanity, alcoholism, abuse, vulgarity, politics and much more. Pandora was frozen in pain and silence. Her beautiful face and body were scarred with poison.

At that very moment King Epimetheus came home from the crusade and slammed down the lid on the only thing that was left in the box . . . Hope.

In Pandora's box of evil, all that remains today is the

quality of hope.

I'm sure you must be very intrigued why I included this story as a summary to a book on business.

One of the greatest payoffs in following the guidelines in "Secrets" is that you will learn to be aware of situations that present themselves cloaked in the illusion of perfection. Wherever you find a situation or a client that is too good to be true, it probably is. Protect yourself. . . .or at least expose the facts and the financial situation behind the motives.

The king accepted his new wife's outward beauty, he did not look any deeper to see her spoiled, immature nature. He did not understand that she was not in love with him, as a man, she was in love with what he could provide for her as king.

Outwardly she presented perfection, inwardly she was self centered, egotistical, and disobedient to the wishes of her husband. Had the king been aware of her qualities, he would have gotten her agreement not to open the box, in writing.

Then he would have had legal recourse.

Had the King exposed her motive in marrying him as a lust for money and power, he would not have married her no matter how beautiful she was.

Finally, the only quality left in Pandora's box that was saved was the treasure of Hope. Hope is an interesting quality, it lives in the future rather than in the present. It bathes the present with the balm of renewal. No matter how difficult or treacherous the situation has been, there is always the promise of new day tomorrow.

If you have uncovered the motives, or financial situation of the client as a Pandora's box of problems, and still feel that you are able to rectify or bring grace to the situation, get the contract in writing. If your skill and experience can change the situation for the benefit of all the parties, proceed with caution, but proceed.

The most important quality you can give anyone who has experienced Pandora's box is the gift of Hope. In the final analysis it is a gift we all deserve.

# Epilogue

## The Chosen Path

The chosen path leads frequently to dead ends. There are often logs or other obstructions across the path. Sometimes there are streams or creeks to jump across. Wildlife appears as we stop to gaze in awe and wonder.

Whether we go on the journey with a full knapsack of supplies, our trail mix of seeds and nuts, appropriate hiking gear and spring water to quench our thirst, are we ready for the adventures that find us?

Whether the journey is for a corporation, an entrepreneur or an individual the secrets are found in the everyday encounters of travellers along the path. The secrets show up in paths that lead to places we don't expect to see. The secrets show up in taking the wrong road. They appear when we least expect them to surprise and delight us.

Taking the path less travelled is necessary for our growth. It leads us to endurance. From suffering in the pain of the mistake, endurance and perseverance have the opportunity to bloom as tiny blossoms in amongst the trees. Where there is endurance, there is growth into character. From character, a corporation, an entrepreneur or an individual finds success. From success, there grow joy and delight. Money shows up to confirm to you that you are in the right place, at the right time.

The secrets are lessons learned along the journey for our amusement and personal change. The lessons teach us at a time when we are ready to learn.

On the stage of life when we finally take our last bow to say thank you for the gift of life and our contribution to it, there is ultimately only an audience of one. The miracle and gift of who you are is all the applause you'll ever need. Carpe diem . . . seize the day, seize the opportunity, seize the miracle of life.

Excellence is your personal journey to fulfillment!

*After Secrets*


*Dedicated to my daughter*
*Who Turned Nineteen*
*This Year*

1. Believe in yourself and your ability to achieve greatness before skill and experience, it's really all you've got. Cherish and nurture this quality of belief.

2. Keep smiling. No matter how long the road to success and the obstacles on the path to excellence, tomorrow is another day.

3. Above all else, remember you are unique and a gift to creation. Use your abilities and talents in the full experience of who you are as a human being.

4. Of all the situations or clients that may disappoint you, there are many, many more that will remain loyal, true blue, and are honest in their employment of your services.

5. The element of risk is involved in all interactions, personal or public. It is your interpretation of the risk and it's impact on your life , that leads to greatness.

6. Cut the strings from your mittens.

7. If there is no partnership or full interaction with the client, the transaction cannot be WIN! WIN!

8. Entrepreneurialism is necessary for growth in all capacities of business.

9. People are motivated to choose productivity for their own benefit first.

10. Enter into all agreements in writing. The parties will appreciate your professionalism and concern for them.

11 Always ask for the order when you like the client. Most salespeople forget to ask. 90% of getting the order is follow-up on lead generation. Thanks to Glenn Ponomarenko.

12. Always be on time—Vince Lombardi time—15 minutes early.

13. Business relationships don't take years to establish, people will either like you or not in the first twenty

minutes of the interview. Remember you are interviewing them to see if you want them in your database forever.

14. Meet clients at your office or theirs. Establish excellence first.

15. Work with clients that are genuinely interested in working with you. Sign contracts when trust has been established. This is not easy for "commitment phobics." They will continue to look for shallow relationships in everything they do. The quality of their personal relationships reflects the quality of their business relationships.

16. Fill up your time when you are without clients by prospecting for them. When you have too many clients to handle, you can be selective about who you decide to work with.

17. Stop calling the client if they don't return you calls or sign a contract. There's tons of business out there for people who are serious about your services or product. Don't respond with anger, continue prospecting, stay nice.

18. Stay professional in all interactions with the client, maintain control. Being social with them is not only unnecessary, it takes time away from your family.

19. It doesn't cost you anything to smile.

20. Once you have a client, remember to appreciate them and say thank you.

21. Management should have real hands on decision making in shaping the values of the organization.

22. Simplify in all areas of organizational structure. Use the KISS method at all times.

23. The world is round. You give in business as in life, you will receive. Give the qualities of truth, honesty,

integrity, excellence; you will be rewarded with a booming business.

24. Keep Hope in all transactions. The client that gives you a small revenue today, could be worth millions tomorrow. Treat him like a CEO before he is one. Every client that gives you a one thousand dollar paycheck is worth over $100,000 in revenues in a lifetime. You only need ten really great, happy clients for a one million dollar income.

25. Keep your clear, compelling vision on dark and dreary days.

26. Hard, tough budgeting builds the cornerstones of success.

27. Ask some one you trust in their experience and wisdom when you run out of answers—the collective community of collaboration always wins.

28. Energy is created and directed when people feel free to contribute in their own capacity for excellence. Recognition and reward build bridges to outstanding results in profits. The water is in your people.

29. Remember there is no greater secret than to love what you do, love your clients and love your company. Your pride will show.

30. Excellence is found in reasonable people who have unreasonable expectations of themselves.

31. Excellence is only heart. You are responsible for the quality of your own life.

32. Excellence is the art of the human soul embodied in the character of work.

33. You are the highest energy. You are the miracle.

# Change has ALWAYS brought opportunity for those who have the courage to act.

Many of those who have purchased "Secrets of Success" have already achieved their desired goals with outstanding and extraordinary results . . . for them, business is booming!

Let me help you turn fear into courage as you apply the principles of proven success. Why not start now, and watch your business take off! Since you are already doing what you love to do, "Secrets of Success in Real Estate Excellence" will only further inspire you to do it in the BEST ways possible.

Make the choice NOW for your future.

Yours with Success,

*Angie Wagner*

## ORDER FORM ————————————————————————————

Name: _____

Address: _____

City: _____

Province/State: _____   Postal/Zip Code: _____

Phone Number: _____   Facsimile Number: _____

| | | |
|---|---|---|
| Secrets of Success Workbook | $29.95 | **METHOD OF PAYMENT** |
| Secrets of Success Tapes Series | | |
| (East) | $159.00 | ☐ Cheque enclosed |
| (West) | $159.00 | ☐ Mastercard / Visa |
| Courage Tape | $10.00 | |
| Purchase any one tape and book | $249.00 | |
| Purchase any two tapes and book | $379.00 | Credit Card Number: |

SUBTOTAL _____

GST _____

PST _____

TOTAL _____

Expiry Date

Signature

MAIL TO:  **DREAMAKERS INTERNATIONAL INC.,**
6850 Millcreek Drive, Mississauga ON   L5N 4J9
Telephone:  (905) 858-3434
Facsimile:  (905) 858-2682

# Are YOU ready for a Miracle with Chiropractic?

Chiropractic is leading the way in the paradigm shift towards whole health. The principled chiropractors and the patients they serve share the same passion for chiropractic, the same love for the healing.
My book "Are You Ready for a Miracle with Chiropractic," is finally being published and ready for sale to your practices and your region. Thank you for all the wonderful stories you contributed.

Yours with Success,
*Angie Wagner*

## ORDER FORM

Name: _____

Address: _____

City: _____

Province/State: _____  Postal/Zip Code: _____

Phone Number: _____  Facsimile Number: _____

Dedication if you wish
book(s) personally
inscribed:

| Number of Copies | Unit Price | Quantity | Total Amt of Order | Add 7% G.S.T. | Add Shipping Charge | Total Payable |
|---|---|---|---|---|---|---|
| 25 or more | $8.00 ea. | | | | $10.00 | |
| 10 to 24 | $10.00 ea. | | | | $5.00 | |
| 1 to 9 | $12.00 ea. | | | | $2.00 | |

### "CREATING THE PRACTICE OF YOUR DREAMS"

Book (CA's)           $29.95  No.___ Total _____ G.S.T. _____ Total_____ Payable_____
3 Audio Tapes (CA's)  $59.95  No.___ Total _____ G.S.T. _____ Total_____ Payable_____

**METHOD OF PAYMENT**

☐ Cash
☐ Cheque enclosed
☐ Mastercard / Visa

Credit Card #_____

Expiry Date _____

Signature _____

MAIL TO:      **DREAMAKERS INTERNATIONAL INC.,**
             6850 Millcreek Drive, Mississauga ON   L5N 4J9
Telephone:    (905) 858-3434
Facsimile:    (905) 858-2682

# NOTES